Praise for *Mastering Resilience Transforming Into Your Purpose* and *Mastering Resilience Workbook*

"Important and informative book. Centered around ACEs (Adverse Childhood Experiences), the author shares her empowering and uplifting insights . . . This is a must-read for those who are trying to overcome adversity."

—*Paula, @pastbookish*

"A trauma survivor herself, Dr. Lorry's advice holds weight. Underscoring her research is something called ACEs, or Adverse Childhood Experiences, that happen between the ages of birth and seventeen years old."

—*Janet @purrfectpages*

"As someone who grew up with childhood trauma, I really found this book useful. I think this would be a great book for adults to read who have suffered through childhood trauma, there is a lot of helpful and useful information to help one heal and to learn to change your mindset."

—*Nicole @reading_with_nicole*

"This book was a fascinating read talking about how childhood traumas (Adverse Childhood Experiences) shape who we are as adults . . . overall, I highly recommend this for teachers and people who work with children, as well as those who need to heal from their own childhood traumas."

—Stefani @that_bookaholic_gal

"I think this book is a great place to learn about ACE. What it is, how it affects a person, and how it can be healed through therapy by applying the simple and practical steps designed by the author, who is a licensed psychologist with expertise in child trauma . . . The binding message of the book, that our adverse experiences eventually make us stronger, and find a purpose that serves to help others and ourselves in a greater context or even a smaller one, was powerful."

—Amber @_readtowrite04_

"Mastering Resilience brings about a lot of self-introspection. It made me stop and think about what could be truly behind some of my actions and how I can address them. The Author has actionable steps & targeted mindset shifts to help the reader."

—Mathi @mowgliwithabook

"Mastering Resilience: Transforming Into Your Purpose by Lorry Leigh Belhumeur, Ph.D., is a valuable resource for people to use to heal and find self-love from their own personal struggles."

—Karen @kmo.reads

"As a high school teacher, I come across students every day from all different backgrounds. Unfortunately, some have difficult home lives and experience trauma at young ages. This book was a great guidebook, providing me with different ways to help them . . . This is a great book for anyone looking to understand what it means to build resilience and positivity in their lives. It's especially helpful to teachers and parents."

—Joanna @joannasbookshelf

"I applaud the author's strength in sharing their story and the stories of those whose lives they have helped to grow and heal. An important read for those looking to overcome adversity in their lives, while also helping to build a better tomorrow. I will definitely try to put some of the things I learned to good use."

—Karen @books.cats.travel.food

"As a nurse and as someone who has personally experienced childhood adversity, this book was truly transformational for me. The recipe and the eight steps help to transform past experience into purpose. Readers will feel empowered to heal and influence future generations— and in helping others, you also help yourself."

—Michelle @nurse_bookie

"*Mastering Resilience* is well written and is an incredible resource for anyone who has experienced childhood adversity or cares for those in this situation."

—Michelle @nurse_bookie

BECOMING
SUPER RESILIENT

BECOMING
SUPER RESILIENT

14 STORIES OF TRANSFORMING ADVERSITY INTO EXTRAORDINARY SUCCESS

Lorry Leigh Belhumeur, Ph.D.

ISBN: 978-1-967703-14-2 - Paperback
ISBN: 978-1-967703-13-5 - Hardcover

Library of Congress Control Number: 2025941319

♾This paper meets the requirements of ANSI/NISO Z39.48-1992 (Permanence of Paper)

Muse Literary Publishing
Send feedback to hello@museliterary.com
Special discounts for bulk sales are available, please contact operations@museliterary.com

0 3 2 6 2 6

Although the world is full of suffering,

it is also full of the overcoming of it.

—Helen Keller

CONTENTS

INTRODUCTION

If you'd told me twenty years ago that I'd be running a multi-million-dollar nonprofit in the social services sector, I'd have laughed. Sure, two decades ago, I'd taken the helm of a nonprofit in the social services sector—but that mental-health nonprofit was in trouble. Unknowingly, I walked into a position where every contract was at risk. We were paid in arrears, and if agencies canceled contracts (which they did), we had already paid team office bills and overhead, forcing the company to draw on a line of credit that left us overextended and financially spiraling. I had a team of five who were overwhelmed, untrained, and under-skilled for the positions they held.

But it's in my nature to fight. To overcome. To see a challenge and pounce.

Our work was providing drastically needed therapy and support to children in our geographic area. Children who'd been neglected, abused, and traumatized—like I'd been. I was determined to turn the ship.

One problem after another was solved until that same nonprofit was healthy and bringing in seven figures a year, with an impact of helping over 100,000 children and families feel emotionally equipped to thrive in life.

Then, we hit a plateau. For about eight years, as we improved our services and grew our team, we were able to maintain our revenue—even during the 2008 economic process, unlike many other nonprofits that went under.

Then, two things happened. First, I used what I had developed to cultivate resilience as a person and a leader of the agency. Then, I began to apply what I'd learned about entrepreneurship, creating entirely new systems, paradigms, and practices for everything from clinical programs, operations, human resources, and marketing.

Breakthrough!

Since then, we've exponentially grown the organization to an eight-figure (now over $30 million) per-year agency, securing multiple multi-year, multi-million-dollar contracts.

When I'm talking with leaders and CEOs, including nonprofits, they ask me how I did it. And inevitably, I talk about what I call "The Mastering Resilience Recipe," not the grueling days and nights in the office (though there were plenty of those).

The pathway I created starts with mindset shifts—elements of a process I developed called "Mastering Resilience." It's the process used to help thousands of people adapt to adversity, and it's the process I used to transform from a psychologist and an entrepreneur into a massively successful leader and bestselling author. And the best part: The recipe works first as a process of personal transformation *(See my book, Mastering Resilience: Transforming Into Your Purpose)* and then can be applied to resilient leadership and business. The work I teach in Super Resilient Leaders helps professionals grow their world-changing missions into an eight-figure impact and income.

This is a book about monumental—and often invisible—shifts. What differentiates a person who's getting by from a person who's thriving? What separates a worker from a leader? What creates a visionary?

I introduced readers to the eight elements of my Mastering Resilience program:

1. **Your BIG Why:** Some call it your vision, your inspiration, the reason you do what you do.

2. **Your Why NOW:** Your commitment, your motivation, and reason for taking action at this time, in this way.

3. **Clarity of Self:** Your deep understanding of who you are— the best version of you, what you stand for, your likes and dislikes.

4. **Cognitive Consistency:** Being aware of your principles, acknowledging their importance, and behaving consistently with them.

5. **Compassion for Self and Others:** Being kind to yourself and to others, even in moments of hurt and pain.

6. **The BOTH Approach:** Speaks to the **cognitive reframing** inherent in reflecting on the positive and negative effects of any situation and using current adversity to grow from past adversity.

7. **Consider the Possibilities:** Your dreams and goals, with course corrections as you strive to stay on track with your dreams and goals. It is your self-awareness reflected in meta-cognitive action.

8. **And Connections and Close Relationships:** The networks that provide you with support, empathy, perspective, guidance, and anything else that allows you to act bravely, successfully adapting to adversity.

I spoke to fourteen individuals who went from adversity to extraordinary success, and whom I'm fortunate enough to know. I wanted to dig deep, to find out where they'd come from and what had happened to them, to understand what motivates and inspires them, and, ultimately, to learn how they'd turned trauma into triumph.

I've worked as a psychologist for more than thirty years. I've heard thousands of clients' stories. And yet these conversations, with some of the people I respect most in the world, moved me to tears and outrage, as well as laughter and joy.

Over and over again, I heard the elements of Mastering Resilience echoing in their stories. Though they may not have used the same terms, they exemplified them. They may have described their vision rather than a BIG Why; maybe they talked about the importance of trusting yourself instead of Compassion. In the end, what they named their points in the process of Mastering Resilience is inconsequential. The actions and attitudes belie a common strength and a universal method for transforming pain into power and purpose. I like to think of Mastering Resilience as a collection of strategies for building resilience; *Becoming Super Resilient* shows those strategies in action.

You'll read about Kenni King, whose institutionalization in a psychiatric hospital inspired her to become a personal growth strategist.

Nigerian-born Enyo Kinney, whose faith and experience growing up in an orphanage motivated her to become a star athlete and personal trainer.

Best-selling author Sara Connell, who overcame sexual abuse and an eating disorder to found a mission-driven company dedicated to helping women use their voice through writing best-selling books and thought leadership.

Donna Kendrick, whose experience with early widowhood led her to a new career as a financial planner specializing in guiding families in transition.

Podcaster and influencer Michelle Thames turned workplace discrimination and racism into an opportunity to develop her own brand and create content for Black women marketers whose experiences weren't reflected in the media.

Serial entrepreneur and data analyst Sheri Chaney Jones overcame self-doubt and depression to launch businesses that solve large-scale societal problems.

Motivated by her own daughter's critical illness, Amanda Hinman became a certified functional medicine health consultant and runs a holistic health practice that empowers women to optimize hormone and gut wellness.

Then there's Marietta Snetsinger, who grew up with a violent sibling and transformed her hypervigilance into a hyper-successful consulting firm.

After yielding to cultural pressures and settling for a loveless marriage, attorney Megha Bhouraskar used her sense of purpose to start a new life—and a new legal practice.

The instability McKenzie Buzard endured in childhood led her to found a hypnotherapy practice that helps people overcome harmful personal narratives.

Certified High Performance Coach Sheryl Kline rose out of a childhood impacted by her mother's mental illness to become an expert in mental toughness and train Olympians and female leaders.

Juliana Garcia Halloran, champion bodybuilder, drew on the support of her close relationships to transcend physical abuse and a toxic relationship.

Best-selling author Andrew Mellen overcame bullying and addiction, and weathered a major career reroute to build an organizing empire.

Finally, Molly Jones' experience growing up closeted paved the way for her forging her own path as an architect, including founding a practice committed to environmental stewardship.

While the lives profiled in these stories couldn't be more different, throughout this book I include reminders about what their experiences share—namely, a high degree of resilience. At the end of each conversation, every person shared their definition of "super resilient," as well as direct advice and encouragement to the reader. You can think of the text boxes with information about the elements from Mastering Resilience as affirmation that the elements work. The page numbers reference the content in the book *Mastering Resilience.*

Resilience Reflections at the end of each chapter create opportunities to contemplate what you want for yourself in life, what actions you can take, and what insights you gain from hearing others' stories.

As I've said, the super-resilient people profiled here talk about their experiences persisting, transforming adversity, and demonstrating grit in all kinds of ways. The language from Mastering Resilience will give you a playbook you can come back to again and again.

Read these stories when you want to be inspired, when you're looking for a way forward, or when you're seeking calm in the storm. Read them and remember your own unique brilliance. But most importantly, read them to embark on your own path—to adapt to the adversity you've faced and come out stronger. More successful. Super resilient.

ONE
I Dare You to Choose Life
Kenni King, Founder of Kenni-Richelle Coaching

At seventeen, Kenni King stood in the bathroom and realized she could no longer lift a toothbrush. Her arms were too weak to comb her hair. She looked into the mirror, frightened. Her face was pale and sunken; her eyes were lost in dark circles.

"I had this romantic relationship with death," she admits. "I was hoping it would come rescue me."

Today, Kenni King is an advocate for herself and others. A personal growth coach and strategist, her work centers around business development from a soul-led, heart-centered place. She helps people redefine success for themselves, creating goals, milestones, and targets based on what makes them happy.

For Kenni, this is profound work. She hopes her clients will, "on their deathbed, look back at their life, proud of what they've overcome, what they've accomplished, and what they're leaving the world with as they go on into whatever's next." But to arrive at a place where she could guide others, she had to confront the person in the mirror.

Once an honor-roll student, cheerleader, singer in choir, and active member of the Lions Club, Kenni had lost all hunger for life. Her parents were divorced, and she grew up splitting her school years between Texas and Arkansas in houses rife with pills and alcohol, shattered glass and broken collarbones, 9-1-1 calls, and blood. By her freshman year of high school, she'd called more than twenty-one different places home. At seventeen, she was crumbling under the strain of relentless stress. Major depressive disorder, anxiety disorder, and chronic insomnia were ravaging her body.

She held on for the younger siblings and kids in her family. Kenni worried about what would happen to her little brother and sister if she weren't there. She felt responsible for showing them the way out by leading herself out. She was the one who tried to shield her brother from the violence and help him with his schoolwork. She was the one who made the kids dinner when there wasn't enough food to put together a full meal—tacos without taco shells, spaghetti without the right sauce— while babysitting. Fueled by love and compassion, she stood in the bathroom and willed herself to act.

"I looked at myself in the mirror and said, 'I dare you, Kenni. I dare you to choose life. It might be harder, but I dare you to make something beautiful out of this brokenness.'"

With the support of a counselor, Kenni spent eleven days in a psychiatric hospital working to balance her meds while taking a break from her environment. It was just enough time to find the will to stay alive.

Upon discharge, she began to focus on health: eating foods that made her feel good, jogging, and finding moments to breathe slowly in the sun. With that new focus, things began to shift. Kenni, a poet and a writer, noticed her friends coming to her with their secrets and fears. She realized that dare she'd made in the bathroom was about more than just staying alive: "The dare was actually about creating the best life possible, one that could positively impact others—and maybe also be the biggest F-you to everybody that hurt me."

After graduating high school (something that had seemed impossible after a senior year with over forty absences), she moved as far away from home as she could. She got a business degree (which she would put to good use) and immediately became a personal trainer.

"I wanted to learn how to help people feel better from the inside out," she says. "Through the journey of personal training, I saw that there were pieces missing." Driven to understand the psychology behind habit change, she transformed personal training into health coaching, and health coaching into life coaching.

Now, after a long path of health, life, advanced transformation, mastery coaching certifications, and experience, Kenni believes in the power of shifting daily habits and internal belief systems to rewrite embedded narratives—even if that means calling on rebellion as a muse.

Growing up, she was told she'd never amount to anything; she'd never have a real career. "I was told that I couldn't break the spell of what was happening in the family," she says. "I wanted to be different. So, there was a sense of rebellion, anger, and rage that also allowed me to go, 'Watch this.'"

Why NOW:

Commitment:
A firm decision—a stake in the ground to do what it takes to heal. Pg. 50.

Today, as a writer, a speaker, and a thought leader, Kenni inspires others to break the spell, too. And as a coach, she pushes her clients to tap into their personal power and do the same. Whether it's mental, physical, or emotional health, spirituality or business, she's an advocate who's passionate about choosing thriving over surviving.

And she gets to support her clients when that professional challenge overlaps with something mortal, something personal: a terminal diagnosis, a death. The fact that Kenni specializes in navigating these moments is a testament to her own commitment to resilience.

"I'm not climbing one mountain," she says. "I'm in a mountain range, and as soon as I get to the top of one, I stop to enjoy the view. Then, I continue to climb onto the next and the next. I choose to keep going. I choose growth and evolution."

That means choosing to keep going, especially during the most difficult moments.

In May 2023, Kenni's father died. The relationship was beyond fraught. Throughout her childhood, he would try to get sober whenever she lived with him, only to relapse.

"He might be sober for two months," she recalls, "and if I left, he would drink again. And that's a really challenging position to be in as a child, even when you're an adult. I was twenty-seven years old when he said, 'Baby doll, you got me sober before. You could do it again.'"

For years, she had wondered how he was still alive, given the decades of alcohol abuse. Even as she worked in therapy with mentors and coaches to process her childhood trauma, she remained in trepidatious contact with him. But when he finally passed away, she found herself flooded with **compassion**, an important element in the Mastering Resilience formula.

"There was that sense of . . . *finally*," she reflects. "But it wasn't about me. The 'finally' was, 'He's no longer in pain.' It was so hard for him to just be alive with his demons in tow and his failing health. His death march was slow, and he is no longer subject to that. He is no longer suffering. He is free."

Suddenly, Kenni saw the hurt, anger, and pain she'd felt related to her father's choices and expectations vanish. And something surprising happened—she began talking to him.

"Out loud," she says, "I was immediately forgiving him. I wanted him to know that there was no baggage left now that he had left his body. It was completely unexpected. I could feel him in the room with me. Now that he could no longer cause me harm, we could have a relationship—a real one. What if death is not an end, but a new beginning? Not just for us when we die, but what if the death of the people that we love signals a new chapter in our relationship versus an end?"

For Kenni, being super resilient calls to mind natural disasters—volcanoes, hurricanes, tsunamis. Amidst decimation and chaos, life still comes back. "It's the same for our grief, trauma, and inner turmoil. Life still comes back, but we must choose it."

Viewing life this way is a decision, and Kenni believes becoming super resilient is a commitment anyone can make. "I believe we decide that we are going to thrive, bloom, blossom, grow, and evolve. And when destruction comes, when we are rocked to our core by devastation, illness, death, traumatic situations—when we allow ourselves to be broken—we gain access to our purest form of power and wake up to our strength."

By calling back that day when she was seventeen, Kenni hopes her story can do what the stories of others did for her. "I remember reading books that were saving my life. I looked to artists, poets, and authors for courage. If they could do it, maybe I could, too. Whatever it is that you can grasp to drive yourself forward, use it. Rebelliousness and rage? Use it. If it's **compassion for others**, because you're not yet in a place where you can fully develop it for yourself, use it."

When coaching her business clients, Kenni often cites the phrase "Build the plane while you're flying it." The same applies to cultivating resilience. "Healing is a lifelong choice. Resilience is a lifelong choice. I'm choosing to take this trash and turn it into treasure. I'm going to make a piece of art from it. I'm going to do something impactful with it. I am choosing to keep going. I'm choosing to stay awake. And, I hope, with my whole heart, you do the same."

> **Do whatever you can to surround yourself with messages of possibility, power, and potential, and you'll go further than you ever thought possible.**
> —Kenni King

Connect with Kenni: https://www.kennirichellecoaching.com/

Author's Note:

During a journey of personal growth and healing, it's critical to make a commitment to the process. In Kenni's case, her commitment to healing was a life-or-death decision.

We make commitments every day. From waking up for that morning meditation and preparing a healthy breakfast, to showing up for our colleagues and having dinner with our families, we make commitments all the time.

Making a commitment to something seems simple. You say you're going to do it, and you do it. Yet if you've ever tried to stick with a New Year's resolution or another goal, you know that making a commitment and keeping it isn't necessarily easy. It takes making course corrections, re-committing when you get off track, and reminding yourself daily of what you are committed to—and why—in order to get the outcome you want. You get to change the way you think.

You've heard the phrase "Change your thinking, change your life." Becoming super resilient requires us to change our thinking.

It's the process of thinking, being, and doing—consistently, intentionally.

How you go about all that is not the most important thing. It's the commitment to the process, insisting on a new mindset for yourself.

If you always do what you always did, you'll get the same result over and over.

Resilience Reflection:

It's time for you to make a commitment. **Say what it is.** Choose one thing that you want to establish in your daily life—one thing you're willing and ready to make a commitment to that will help you become super resilient. Make that commitment right here, right now.

In your journal (or even in the margin), jot down what result you want for yourself. **Write it down.** What will you achieve when you go **ALL IN** on your commitment to yourself? What exactly is your desired outcome?

You may be considering big commitments—choosing life, like Kenni did: quitting smoking, releasing weight, or living in gratitude. Or, your commitments could be smaller: making your bed every day, taking a ten-minute rest break, or leaving your phone in the other room during family movie night. Whatever the magnitude of your commitment, make it now!

Take a few minutes to imagine three scenarios.

Scenario 1: It's thirty days from now, and you're celebrating, You did it! You went all in and wholly committed. You stuck to your commitment, and now people are noticing. What are you feeling? What are you thinking? Are you viewing yourself any differently? Think about your outcome and congratulate yourself. Give yourself time to let this experience sink in and feel good.

Scenario 2: It's thirty days from now, and you made the same commitment . . . only halfway through the process, you got off track. You gave it a shot. You started off strong and gradually broke the commitment to yourself. What are you feeling? What are you thinking? Are you viewing yourself any differently? Give yourself time to let this experience sink in, and witness what you're feeling.

Scenario 3: It's thirty days from now, and you made the same commitment on day one—but that's the end of the story. You didn't take any action, though you may have found yourself thinking about your commitment plenty. You were serious about that commitment! You had good intentions. At this moment, what are you feeling? What are you thinking? Are you viewing yourself any differently? Give yourself time to let this experience sink in, and observe what you're feeling.

Now that you've imagined these three scenarios, it's time to choose. Decide for yourself which outcome you're committed to and which scenario you want to realize. Remember the feeling when you went **ALL IN**. Make *that* commitment today.

*You'll find a companion version of this activity in the *Mastering Resilience Workbook* on page 14.

TWO
Training for Good
Enyo Kinney, Personal Trainer

Thinking about our impact on future generations comes naturally to Enyo Kinney, even if she hasn't always been a star athlete and a fitness pro.

She was born and raised in Nigeria. Over thirty years ago, as newlyweds, her parents founded an orphanage. "They're the most remarkable and selfless people I've ever met," Enyo says. "They started this thing that they felt called to do."

Today, the orphanage houses more than five hundred people. On that compound, Enyo grew up, sleeping apart from her biological sisters. "I slept in the same dorm as people my age," she says. "We didn't know any better. We just thought, 'That's our life.' I grew up with a lot of siblings playing together."

With that many children to take care of, there wasn't money for organized sports or private school. Enyo spent her days playing games of soccer or attending homeschool with her "brothers and sisters."

When she was fourteen, Enyo received a scholarship to attend a high school in Canada. Her biological siblings were in the United States, and she was eager to be closer to them. Her parents told her they would pray for her, and off she went.

Enyo had never been on a plane. She'd never flown. She wasn't used to Canadian winters. And she wasn't accustomed to English. "We spoke English at home," she says, "but I had to really listen to understand English in the classroom." Enyo would pray the teacher wouldn't call on her; she feared people making fun of her speech.

Beyond the language barrier, figuring out how to exist in Canada, in the particular culture of the school was difficult. "The first couple of months were rough. It was a boarding school, and I was thrown in with students who knew a lot of English and were rich kids. I came from a family where there was no way I could've afforded that school if it wasn't for the scholarship."

It took her a year to acclimate—to learn how to be so far from her parents, to feel confident speaking up in school. But Enyo grew. "By the time I left, I thought I knew everything," she laughs. "I was so thankful for the experience."

When she graduated from high school, Enyo Kinney decided to become a track athlete. There was just one tiny complication—she'd never run competitively.

"Rugby, soccer, field hockey—I loved all of that," Enyo says. "But then I said I wanted to pursue running, which sounded crazy at the time. I didn't run in high school. How do you run as a team athlete in college?"

Enyo took a year off. She moved to Colorado, worked part-time, and walked to the nearest school track. She followed online workouts and connected with a coach. The next fall, she arrived at Minnesota State University, Mankato after contacting the coach and asking to be a part of the team—without having competed. The coach agreed to let her join, and Enyo went on to run on 4x4s, 60-meters, 400-meters, and everything in between on conference-winning teams.

Today, Enyo Kinney is a personal trainer based in Orange County, CA. While she focuses on directing clients' workout programs and helping them meet their immediate goals—whether that's building muscle mass, reducing body fat, or safely rehabilitating after surgery—she also believes in reminding them that physical fitness is about more than hitting a certain weight, wearing a certain size, or looking good at a big event.

"This is for your health," says Enyo. "This is for your kids' health and your grandkids' health. We all know working out is good in the here and now, but what I really focus on is the long-term and what I can do to help people understand that."

The BOTH Approach:

An element of this approach—cognitive reframing—is assigning meaning and purpose to every experience we have. We are stronger individually because of the adversities. Pg. 109

Enyo's past experiences prepared her for a current challenge—being a military wife. Enyo met her husband at an athlete's Bible study her first week at college; they married three weeks before graduation. These days, she finds herself moving around frequently (from Minnesota to Virginia to California) and enduring long absences.

"My husband has been deployed for the past five months, and he's still on deployment for the next two. The time apart is hard, but the hardest thing is just knowing the work he's doing. When I pray, I am at peace knowing that God is taking care of him. I don't have any control over it."

Leaving home at a young age, Enyo's faith grew. Faith helped her trust that her family was well when she was in high school, and faith helps her believe in her husband's safety when he's on deployment. It's what kept her grounded before track meets, too.

"I'll think, 'God, I've worked hard. This is all in your hands.'" This peace of mind helps Enyo navigate challenges. "When things don't go the way I want them to, I always know that it is God's will. I live a very free life. We're humans—I still worry about stuff, but at the end of the day, I lay down in bed knowing that everything is out of my control."

Now, Enyo is preparing for another season of moves based on her husband's assignment. There will be the usual challenges—learning a new city, making friends, and re-establishing herself professionally. But she has faith that she'll thrive, and that's something she tries to teach her clients.

"How are you going to train your body if you're not going to train your mind? Restarting is something I've realized is going to be a part of my life for a long time."

It's this kind of **cognitive reframing** that's one of the most important steps in Mastering Resilience; it's one of the reasons Enyo is so super resilient.

Enyo remembers her first weeks living in California. She had a moment of feeling sorry for herself. Here she was, having to start all over again. "The first week, I was homesick," she admits, "but then I was like, 'Go for a run on the beach.' And as soon as I did that, I started to appreciate this place."

To Enyo, "Being super resilient means finding things that make whatever situation you're in better. It means having the ability to recover from tough things. And knowing it's not ever just a hard season of life, and it's not ever just an easy season of life. It's often both." Her advice to people who want to become super resilient stems from her childhood. "My dad always taught us that, if somebody is mean to you, look for the one percent good in them. Give them the benefit of the doubt. We're not meant to be happy twenty-four seven. And know, whatever situation you're in is not forever. It will pass."

> **Being super resilient means finding things that make whatever situation you're in better.**
> **—Enyo Kinney**

Connect with Enyo: https://www.instagram.com/fit.with.enyo/

Author's Note:

Enyo endured and now thrives in the face of the many adversities in her life. She acknowledged the reality of her challenges while being intentional, taking action, and focusing on positive things that her future holds.

This is, at its core, cognitive reframing—assigning meaning to what you encounter with a positive outlook—things from the past, the present, and the future.

Cognitive reframing is a common thread and the most mentioned element of becoming super resilient. It's the ability to interpret adversities positively, to assign meaning and purpose to every experience we have.

It's natural to feel broken when you've faced childhood or other adversities. In fact, you might feel irreparably broken. You may have experienced a lack of confidence, feeling stuck, or blaming yourself for the unfortunate things that have happened to you and in your life. It's easier to have unpleasant thoughts; it's easier to assign negative meaning to situations and outcomes.

Failing at something might have meant "I'll never be good at it; I'll never be successful." Losing a client meant, "I suck at business," and losing your temper meant "I'm a terrible person." Assigning this type of negative meaning to outcomes—or wishing the past had been different—doesn't serve you. It's unhelpful at best and damaging at worst. You can't change your past, but you can think differently about it.

Thinking about the good that came out of adversity allows you to become grounded, more productive, and experience a more meaningful life (viewing adversity in a positive light is different from toxic positivity).

Every challenging experience presents an opportunity to think of something good that came out of it. Having a big heart and caring deeply for others, feeling empathy toward people who've faced similar adversities, relating to others without judgment—all of these traits could have driven you toward your profession. Maybe you adapted to childhood chaos by becoming an organized and driven adult. As a direct response to adversity, you might very well have the attitude of, "Just watch me!"

If you're reading this book, chances are you can recall difficult situations when you assigned negative meaning, as well as those when you were able to reframe. Perhaps you've seen how reframing served you and helped you move forward. Giving positive meaning to these challenges results in optimism and hope.

Resilience Reflection:

Allow yourself a minute to think about a situation when you were able to view the good that came out of it, even though it was unpleasant at the time. It might have been a breakup that paved the way for a better relationship, the loss of a job that catapulted you to a better career path, or an injury that slowed you down when that's exactly what you needed.

What's yours? As you think about the positive outcomes, pay attention to your feelings, the expression on your face, and your overall perspective on the situation. What do you notice?

For a brief second, allow yourself to recall an unpleasant situation where you dwelled on the negative. Is it possible for you to see the good that came out of it when you put your mind to it? Take this opportunity to challenge your thinking about the situation or outcome, and frame it in a way that is helpful and serves you, no longer damaging your psyche. Pay attention to your feelings and any tension in your body. Does anything shift as you seek out the positive?

This is a strategy you can use anytime you catch yourself dwelling on the negative. The sooner you shift your view from negative to positive, the sooner you'll have a more hopeful and optimistic outlook—critical to becoming super resilient.

THREE
Follow the Breadcrumbs
Sara Connell, Founder of
Thought Leader Academy

Sara Connell was working at one of the top ad agencies in the US. A recent graduate of Northwestern, she had been excited to get a job in a creative field at a company recognized as a top workplace for women.

"I quickly learned there was a lot of institutionalized sexual abuse and sexual assault," Sara says. "I felt trapped. None of the authority figures were going to create boundaries or protection. I'd recreated my childhood at the workplace."

Since adolescence, Sara had managed trauma—rape, molestation, more—by eating. Or, more often, not eating. Starvation and other behaviors, which she recognized as symptoms of an eating disorder, were progressing. There were physical and mental signs that she was sick and getting sicker. She had stopped sleeping, and that scared her the most. "I understood I would die if I continued down this road."

One day, in the midst of all this, Sara found herself traveling from Boston to Chicago. She wandered into an airport bookstore and picked up *Holy Hunger: A Woman's Journey from Food Addiction to Spiritual Fulfillment* by Margaret Bullitt-Jonas. She bought the book, got on the plane, started reading—and continued reading all night.

"I call it the book that saved my life," Sara says. "I gave a TEDx talk on it. Even though Bullitt-Jonas' story was different than mine, she shared what she did to get better. And I was like, 'That's it. I can't live like this anymore.' I knew I had to wake up from all that."

This was a **Why NOW** moment for Sara, a commitment that serves as the motivation to keep going, to do whatever it takes to continue the healing journey.

Sara Connell is a writer and the founder of Thought Leader Academy, where she helps coaches, writers, and entrepreneurs become successful, published authors, and in-demand speakers getting on stages and monetizing their missions. She has been featured on *The Oprah Winfrey Show*, *Good Morning America*, *The View*, FOX Chicago, TEDx, *The Today Show*, and *Katie Couric*. Her writing has appeared in *The New York Times*, *Forbes*, *Good Housekeeping*, and *Parenting*. The author of five books, she has been nominated for a national book award and *ELLE* magazine Book of the Year.

After Sara's wake-up call, she quit her job. "I had no plan," she admits. "I just knew I had to get help." She went into recovery for the eating disorder, and shortly thereafter, her then fiancée got an opportunity to move to London.

Unable to obtain a work visa until the marriage was official, Sara undertook work of her own—emotional work. Spiritual work. "It was the biggest gift ever," she says. "I had nine months before we got married, and I just went into deep, intensive trauma treatment. I used every method. There was therapy and shamans, all kinds of cool stuff."

All the while, she was writing.

"It sucked," Sara laughs. "I didn't know what I was doing."

An English major in college, Sara had never taken creative writing courses. And yet, she was drawn to writing. "I wrote a novel manuscript that's never seen the light of day," she shares. "It was fun, a great practice book."

A few online writing workshops later, Sara connected with her agent, who's still her agent today. That agent gave Sara edits on the memoir that would land her her first book deal, *Bringing in Finn: An Extraordinary Surrogacy Story*.

Telling her own story—of the grueling fertility ordeal that ended in her sixty-one-year-old mother carrying Sara's child—made her feel like she'd made it as a writer (appearing on *Oprah* didn't hurt). But Sara knew she wanted to help other women amplify their voices, too.

Growing up, she'd always been told she was too much—too outspoken, too boisterous, too everything. Having spent a decade trying to shrink herself by starving and then getting to a place of recovery, Sara knew she wanted to help other women let go of the oppressive, silencing forces in their lives. Here was her **BIG Why**, the inspiration for what she does. She trained as a coach.

"It's important to me that women get to use their voice in the ways that they want to use it. That matters so deeply to me, I think, because it was so squashed for me as a child. Ninety-nine percent of my clients come in and have some version of imposter syndrome, some version of 'I'm not good enough,' some version of 'Who'd want to hear from me,' but yet they have this flame that's been lit around something they're here to share. For me, it's about releasing those bondages so they can share in whatever form they choose to share it in."

Sara began book coaching and soon realized that, for many people, the book isn't the ultimate goal. And she noticed something in herself shifting, too. "The Buddhists call it the pregnant void," Sara says. "It's this sense—it can be very uncomfortable—that something's changing."

After a few months of soul searching, Sara decided it was time to combine her training and experience—"in coaching, and mindset, and neuroscience, and peak performance, and supporting people in their personal development"—and establish the Thought Leader Academy (TLA), an incubator for women change-makers. Publishing is one pillar of TLA; from there, Sara says, "Other components come together and create a legacy that people want to create—speaking, building an audience, and creating other products, or programs, or services that go along with the thought leadership and drive revenue."

While talking about revenue may linger as a cultural taboo, Sara believes it's especially important for women and people who've experienced Adverse Childhood Experiences (ACEs) to reframe the stories they tell themselves about money.

"I think there's an enormous correlation between childhood trauma and earning," she shares. "That's what I was for so long. Even when I started just helping people with books, I couldn't take care of myself financially very well. It was a struggle for a long time. And it took doing a lot of work, a lot of neuroscience-based treatment, to adopt a new language of being profitable, successful, and prosperous—all those things that were bad in my family."

And in her sixth book, Sara adopts another new language: writing about thought leadership. Despite her success (*LA Weekly* named her one of the top five entrepreneurs in 2023), she was hesitant to "do a book about business. I wasn't as passionate," she admits, until I said, "What I want to get into is the neuroscience. Reframing the narrative. Our stories are destiny. When I was running the 'You're not good with money, you're broken, you're a bad person' story, that's exactly what I was experiencing. I love neuroplasticity because we can rewrite the narrative and experience something new."

This peek into Sara's writing process shows how important it is to know your true self and rewrite the story with the best version of yourself in mind.

Clarity of Self:

Clarity of Self is so important for resilience because knowing your true identity and taking actions consistent with that identity supercharges your healing journey. Pg. 67

So, what does "super resilient" mean to Sara? Not surprisingly, she offers a story (starring two saucy angels).

"When I was fifteen, my left ovary ruptured. It was very scary. Excruciatingly painful. And my parents wouldn't take me to the hospital. They thought I was being dramatic. When I finally got to the hospital, they had to do emergency surgery. Around that time, the eating disorders really kicked in. It was just like, 'I'm not safe. My body's not safe here.'"

As an adult, Sara did Eye Movement Desensitization Reprocessing (EMDR) therapy, working through that experience in the hospital. "In my narrative, it was always, 'I almost died. I almost died. It was so scary.' During EMDR, a new perspective came in. I had an image of these angels—and I'm not a big angel person. I had this image of these angels sitting and watching over the surgery, and they were both like, 'Yeah, you look pretty good to me.' I was thirty-something, and it was so awesome to be called out on this victim narrative."

Being super resilient, in other words, is not buying into the "everything's going to kill me" story. It's believing "I have a pretty strong life force."

For people working toward Mastering Resilience, Sara has advice. (And yes, it works for writing, too.)

"Everything is revisable," she says, "all the messages that you're broken or defective. Everything is healable, everything. Your antidote is right where you are. The answer that you need, whatever the modality, the person, the book, whatever it is, is at hand. Whatever nudge from the universe, whatever book falls off the shelf, whatever thing you've heard about, that weekend workshop or whatever, that nudge could be useful. Just take that next step, and just follow the breadcrumbs."

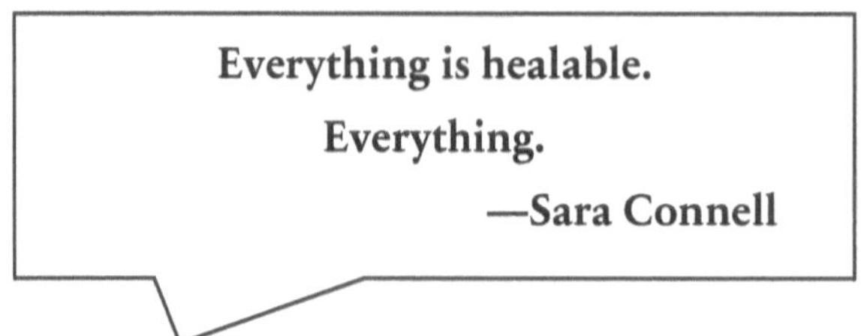

Connect with Sara: https://www.saraconnell.com/

Author's Note:

Sara used several strategies on her journey to becoming super resilient—including establishing her **BIG Why** and her **Why NOW**—but the one that stands out to me is her relentless pursuit of finding her authentic self, being honest with herself when she needed help, and getting it. Developing this **Clarity of Self** was an integral part of her journey. Today, she knows her true self and her calling, and is not swayed by what others told her she was. Sara is crystal-clear about who she gets to be to help others bring purpose into their lives.

As Socrates said, "Know thyself." Knowing our strengths as well as our setbacks, our qualities and characteristics, our likes and dislikes, is all part of the process of developing and having **Clarity of Self**.

I love music; music moves me. I love to sing. And yet, I know I'm not a good singer. I wish I was. When I was in third grade, I was the narrator in a play, as well as playing the part of a sarcastic girl. The part required me to sing one line, intentionally off-key. Maybe I didn't connect the dots at the time, but the director who cast me knew me better than I knew myself. I was a gifted storyteller . . . and a lousy singer! She saw my strengths better than I did. (That happens.)

Clarity of Self: being clear about your likes and dislikes, your values, qualities, strengths, and setbacks, as well as believing in your intrinsic worth. This is an important aspect in becoming super resilient. When you know precisely who you are, others can't convince you otherwise—even if they try. When you are grounded and rooted in self-love, no one can take that from you. You set better boundaries. You don't care about what others think or say about you, because it's none of your business. You are focused and moving toward your dreams and goals, stepping into who you get to BE along the way.

Knowing who you are and who you've become helps guide your decisions and actions in the face of adversity. When you're influenced by what other people say about you or circumstances derail you, being clear about who you are and your value helps you get on track more quickly.

Resilience Reflection

Take a few moments to get grounded in your **Clarity of Self** right now. Reflect on the following questions:

- Who do you think you ARE?
- Who do you say you are?
- Who do your loved ones say you are?

- Who do you get to BE to achieve your dreams and goals? Think about the qualities and characteristics that are required of you in order to get there.

Now imagine your future self, the you that's achieved the next big accomplishment. Imagine all the talents, skills, and strengths that have gotten you to this point. Take one action today in alignment with your future/true self. Celebrate the person you know yourself to be.

How has being clear on who you get to be helped you achieve that goal?

Yes, your answers to these questions might change over time. We constantly learn new things about ourselves.

Answering these questions may seem like it takes a while, yet you can have **Clarity of Self** at any point. We learn new things about ourselves all the time.

FOUR
Be Your Own Best Friend
(and Other Ways to Value Yourself)
Donna Kendrick, Founder of Sephton Financial and Host of Widow, Wisdom & Wealth

Donna Kendrick grew up in a cozy Philadelphia enclave of firefighters and police officers, where everyone looked out for one another. That's how she met her husband, Greg—he was the son of a Philly cop. With a degree in statistics for business from Penn State, Donna had a career in financial forecasting for the pharmaceutical industry. Greg worked for the Department of Homeland Security. When Greg was positioned abroad, the family moved to Rome, babies in tow. After her third child, Donna gave up her career—Greg's second appointment at the embassy effectively demanded it.

"I wound up teaching English to Italian kids." She laughs. "My joke is they all pronounce water 'warder.'"

The family spent years moving around with Greg's career until 2013, when he was positioned in Philadelphia. Donna was relieved. She began settling in the suburbs and reconnecting with their old community. After living like a military family, here was home, surrounded by family and friends. "We moved into my sister's school district," Donna says. "I thought, 'Hey, my kids are learning to speak English.'"

Then, Greg died by suicide.

Donna was blindsided. Her children were eight, eleven, and twelve. She was making $17,000 a year as a teaching assistant. Yet, she says, "I counted myself blessed and lucky. My husband and I had a financial planner in our twenties before we moved abroad. And that financial advisor got us the life insurance policy that covered me when he passed."

Donna Kendrick is the founder of Sephton Financial, a financial planning and asset management firm that specializes in families in transition—widowhood, divorce, or career change. She's the author of the number-one Amazon bestseller *A Guide to Widowhood: Navigating the First Three Years*, a book which spawned public speaking opportunities, a virtual course, and, most recently, the podcast *Widow, Wisdom &*

Wealth. In addition to being a Certified Financial Planner and a Certified Divorce Financial Analyst, she's also a trained Grief Recovery Method specialist.

"Whatever I do, I make sure it's in line with my mission," Donna says. "And my mission is really to help families in transition take their next right step."

When Greg died, Donna found herself in a situation that she'd come to see as remarkable: "I was able to keep my house and educate my kids. Not many widows and widowers wind up better financially after their spouse passed."

But this was temporary—benefits like pension and social security would run out, and supporting her family on a teacher's assistant salary was unrealistic. She knew she had to take her own next right step.

"I had to relaunch my career."

Before tackling something as monumental as a professional rebirth, Donna set goals to help her family. "I gave the kids one week. Then they went back to school. I don't know if I did that right or wrong." She thought it was best for them to get back to life.

By her third year of widowhood, Donna achieved clarity on her life's mission. "Life gave me lemons," she said. "I would make lemonade. I wasn't going to go back to working full full-time with anything that didn't make a change out of it all."

Donna went to her financial advisor—someone she'd been using since Greg's death, someone who fit her needs as a widow. She sat down with him and explained her goal. "'I want to do what you did for me for other people,'" she recalls saying. "'How do I do it?' He gave me a framework of the education I needed. He mentored me, and I was off and running."

Donna went back to school and completed her licensing. By 2020, she'd hung her own shingle and begun establishing her niche in the marketplace. "While I was getting my feet wet, I was a generalist. Soon, I really started saying, '*This* is what I specialize in—families in transition, families that need a lot of education so that I can protect them the way our financial advisor did for me and Greg.'"

Consider the Possibilities:

When you become open (and stay open), to consider new possibilities, you allow the right people, situations, and paths to come into your life easily and graciously. Pg. 135.

Setting goals and charting a course for her life has motivated Donna for as long as she can remember. As a child, she recognized that she was hyper. "It was hard and painful to sit still in school." Still, she knew good grades were important to her parents, that they were making sacrifices for her education (her father worked as a janitor on his days off of firefighter shifts; her mother worked in the library), so she figured out how to focus. "It didn't come easy. But I knew how to rein myself in to accomplish the goal."

When her parents divorced, her mother remarried. Donna's stepfather and her new stepbrother were abusive, and her mother wouldn't let her move out because the family needed the child support payments.

"I had a dollar sign on my head. Not good. When I turned eighteen, I decided I was done. I wasn't coming home. It was natural to go away to school, and I knew in the back of my mind, I wasn't coming home for breaks." She took it step-by-step, laying the groundwork, figuring out which friend's parents she could stay with over Thanksgiving.

"I've always had a really good faith in me being able to figure it out," Donna says. "I was surviving on my own at eighteen, getting a job, and moving away at twenty-one. By twenty-one, I had rent, a job, benefits—I was contributing to my 401k. Those early lessons as a teenager or being on my own as a young adult—and proud of it—made me feel so capable after Greg passed."

Helping others navigate grief efficiently and capably is an important part of Donna's life. After going through the Grief Recovery program after Greg's death, she trained to become a certified Grief Recovery

Specialist herself. Now she runs four eight-week Grief Recovery courses a year, two in-person and two over Zoom.

"It's my payback to the community," says Donna. "It addresses forty different ways that you could lose anything. My parents lived together while separated in a house, and I saw their behavior. As a kid, that's what I was influenced by. How did that experience influence how I dealt with my own kids right after their dad passed? Realizing how that impacts you is what the Grief Recovery Method is."

Donna's fortitude and self-awareness are remarkable; so is her ability to **cognitively reframe** her thinking, even in the hardest circumstances. "When Greg passed, it was horrible." Eventually, she says, "I could take the big deep breath and be like, 'Kids, we're going to be all right.'"

Today, Donna is the proud mom of a blended family. She lives in Pennsylvania with her new husband, Jim, and their six children. And she understands, every day, what it means to be super resilient. "What you're experiencing right now will, down the line, build a better life for you and your family, those you love. Being super resilient means keeping that at the back of your mind, no matter how much it hurts. I'm not saying ignore the pain. I'm not saying ignore the feeling, but know there's a pot of gold at the end of the rainbow."

Donna advises people Mastering Resilience to practice the **cognitive**

reframing she's found so useful in her own life, especially when they're going through a difficult experience. "Ask, 'What can I pull out of this? What can I make positive out of it?' Of course, trusting yourself to find meaning or see the silver lining requires, well, just that—trusting yourself. Valuing yourself."

And that's Donna's most urgent suggestion.

"Be your own best friend," she urges. "You always have those little gremlins in the back of your head. You always have your thought process and quiet moments. It's you and your soul. That's the communications. That's where progress happens. That's where you find the next step for resiliency."

> **Be your own best friend. It's you and your soul. That's where progress happens. That's where you find the next step for resiliency.**
> **—Donna Kendrick**

Connect with Donna: https://sephtonfinancial.com/

Author's Note:

When tragedy struck and Donna lost her husband, she was determined to make a change. She knew that, despite the pain and grief she and her family were facing, this was the moment to restart her career. For years, she'd set aside her own professional ambition to support her husband's work while raising their children. Like many women, her own goals took a backseat to the family's priorities.

And yet, Donna never forgot that she was someone goal-driven. As she helped her family rebuild their life, she imagined how she might give meaning to her mourning. From seeking mentorship from the financial advisor who helped her grow her own financial security to training as a Grief Recovery Counselor, Donna never stopped envisioning new possibilities for her future.

Considering the Possibilities is an important element of becoming super resilient. What does it mean to **Consider the Possibilities?** It goes beyond dreaming or envisioning. It's being open to staying open. It's allowing yourself the freedom to imagine a path forward, even when you don't know exactly where that path will lead. When you **Consider the Possibilities** and you're open, you'll find people and circumstances around you that can be instrumental in helping you achieve your goals.

For Donna, considering the possibilities helped her gain clarity on her purpose. By being open to being open, she saw that her desire to do meaningful work with families who'd endured circumstances akin to her own would take her down a new career path—and enable her to give back.

Of course, it's not always easy to **Consider the Possibilities**. When you're going through a challenging situation or dealing with serious adversity, you may be accustomed to living with your breath held, waiting for the other shoe to drop. Daydreaming about the future might seem like a waste of time.

And yet, being open to staying open can be a radical act of self-salvation, a lifeline. What if you imagined that the other shoe didn't drop? What could happen instead? Your brain will pay attention to what it thinks is important. The more you **Consider the Possibilities**, the more your brain will look for them . . . and the more you'll find them.

Resilience Reflection:

Close your eyes and allow yourself to imagine something you'd love to be doing in the future or a characteristic you want to embody. You might dream of climbing Mount Kilimanjaro, or starting your own business, or taking up pickleball. You might dream of being more joyful or more lighthearted. Take a few moments to consider your possibilities.

Now jot down: What would it mean for you to be open to being open—to believing that anything is possible (in a good way)? How would you feel? How would that sense of receptivity change how you move through the day? What are you seeing and experiencing?

This action is endlessly repeatable. After all, becoming super resilient is an ongoing journey.

FIVE
You Are Meant to Help More People
Michelle Thames, Founder of
Thames Media Solutions, LLC

In 2016, Michelle Thames was working in health administration. As a compliance coordinator at a large county hospital, her days consisted of receiving bills, paying bills, and managing the hospital's education system. She hoped to one day become a compliance officer—after all, she had a BA and an MHA in health administration. Outside the office, she shared her love of beauty and haircare products on a blog called *Happily Ever Natural.*

"I didn't know there was this whole community of women just like me going through their natural hair journey, growing out our relaxer so our natural curls could flourish," says Michelle. "I didn't have any idea about blogging or being a creator. I really just jumped in."

Blogging was a side hustle, a creative outlet Michelle explored when she wasn't working. Then, after only six months in her position at the hospital, she was fired.

At the time, she was shocked. She liked the job; she knew she was performing above expectations. She had no idea why she'd been fired until, four years later, a lawyer contacted her.

"I got fired because I was Black," Michelle says. "The lawyer asked if I could tell him about my firing because he had a client—also a Black woman—who'd been wrongfully fired. I told him my story. When I finished, he was astonished. It was the exact same story of his client. The woman who fired me had been doing this to other people."

As angry as she was, Michelle reflected on those events with **compassion** and self-confidence. "The woman who fired me has to deal with her demons or whatever," she says. "It wasn't about me. It was about her and her beliefs. I wasn't going to let that break me. Getting fired was a major tragedy that I turned into a triumph."

Today, Michelle Thames is a marketing and monetization strategist. The co-founder of Thames Media Solutions, LLC, a boutique marketing agency, Michelle is a blogger and influencer, as well as the host of the podcast *Social Media Decoded*. She's passionate about teaching creators, influencers, and small-business owners how to build strategies to market their brands on social media, to increase their reach and their revenue. The Chicago native is a devoted wife and mother.

Though Michelle was blindsided by losing her job, she took it as a sign. Maybe healthcare wasn't aligned with what she wanted to do. Being fired let her explore her passions and dive into her side hustle. From there, she began to freelance.

"I freelanced for a popular beauty site, and really got my feet wet with writing," she says. "I put myself out there."

Soon, she connected with an up-and-coming beauty brand looking for someone to run their social media. Today it's a multimillion-dollar company, and Michelle played a pivotal role in building the social media foundation of their brand.

While she loved growing a business from its startup stage, Michelle felt a deeper urge to do something bigger. "God was saying, 'This is the company's dream . . . which is great. But you are meant to help more people.'"

Cognitive Consistency:

Behaving consistently with your values and in the direction of your dreams and goals. Be aware of your thoughts, acknowledge your true value, and take actions consistent with your true identity. Pg. 81.

Michelle was aware of her passion for marketing. She acknowledged that she wanted to do something more. And she took decisive action.

Four years ago, Michelle left the beauty company to start her own marketing agency with her husband, and her influence in the world of marketing has been expanding ever since.

"This whole journey," she says, "has been a testament to how you can pivot."

Michelle wasn't always this confident. Growing up, she made friends easily, never fitting in with one given clique. When she was in high school, the family moved, and Michelle had to start at a new school. She tried to establish new relationships, but it wasn't always easy to feel accepted. Case in point: the talent show.

"Me and two other girls got up on stage and performed 'Survivor' by Destiny's Child. We got booed by the whole entire school. And that crushed me—I don't think the kids really understood what that did. Can you imagine if it was today, with social media? Luckily, we didn't have social media back then, so it blew over, but after that, I decided I never wanted to feel that way again. I could control to a certain extent how I was perceived in the world. From thereon out, I said, 'You know what? I'm going to stand tall on these stages.'"

Even if those stages are metaphorical. With her podcast *Social Media Decoded*, Michelle gets to share her marketing insights and interview experts from all over the world. In the podcast's 280 episodes, she's committed to teaching marketing in bite-size lessons, breaking things down into "really great gems you can implement. The reason I created the podcast," she shares, "is I wanted to be seen as a thought leader and an expert."

And while the podcast is another tool in her own marketing arsenal, it addresses something profoundly important to Michelle. "I created my podcast because I didn't see enough Black women. I didn't see enough Black women marketers. It's a male-dominated industry. How do you break through that? With the background I have and the credibility I have, I was just like, 'It's either go hard or go home. Really put yourself out there.'"

By putting herself out there, Michelle's community has grown.

"I started building an audience fourteen years ago," she reflects. "So, a lot of people who follow me have been following me for the last fourteen years. They've seen all the changes that I've been through. That community has been one of the things that has uplifted me, that has kept me going. When you get messages from people and they say, 'This inspired me,' it keeps me fueled to continue."

And for Michelle, continuing—as much as consistency—is key. For her, being super resilient means being able to bounce back . . . from anything. "There are so many things that get thrown at us," she says. "Sickness, disease, death. I've been through it all. So to keep going, no matter what, that's what it means to be super resilient."

To be sure, Michelle's confidence and inner strength make her super resilient—after all, she says, "From that time I got fired, I wasn't going to let my destiny be in anybody else's hands."

Still, she's quick to share the importance of others in motivating her. "My family definitely keeps me going. And God—because faith is real. And if I didn't have faith in something, there's no way that I would even be able to get through this. You choose, but you have to believe in something."

And Michelle believes in the power of people to transform their own lives, whether it's through social media marketing or Mastering Resilience. She has advice. "When you're going through changes and you're becoming more resilient, people may look at you differently. Whatever they think about you is their problem, like the woman who fired me—it's her problem, and it's okay. You can continue to move forward no matter what. If you don't care what other people say about you, you can be resilient in anything. You'll just keep going."

> **Your downfalls are stepping-stones to something better.**
> —**Michelle Thames**

Connect with Michelle: https://thamesmediasolutions.com/

Author's Note:

Michelle was shocked when she was fired from her job at the hospital. She knew she was a high performer, she knew she was beyond competent, and she knew she knew the job. And yet, Michelle took this tragedy and turned it into a triumph, following her dream to take her blogging to the next level—and then some.

It always strikes me when I see people exhibiting the behaviors and strategies integral to Mastering Resilience in their own lives. After all, in developing my course, I reverse-engineered what worked. What Michelle displays is **Cognitive Consistency**.

People are motivated by the desire to change inconsistencies. We want to have consistency. We want our behaviors and actions to be consistent with our thoughts. This is the principle behind **Cognitive Consistency.**

Without knowing it, Michelle was applying a core strategy of Mastering Resilience: the **AAA**s of Mastering Resilience. Be **a**ware, **a**cknowledge, and take **a**ction.

Since Michelle was so confident, she was driven to act accordingly.

Michelle found herself in a situation where there was disconnect between her sense of herself and her employer's. She was **aware** of the inequity of the situation. She **acknowledged**, too, that she was a stellar employee; she was confident in her work and performance.

With that sense of self rooted in her mind, she couldn't stay there; she shifted the work she was doing, knowing that her true calling was waiting for her elsewhere. By taking **action**, she soared, taking the next best step toward her dreams and goals.

The **AAA**s come after the **BIG Why** and the **Why NOW**, and after **Clarity of Self**. You've identified what inspires you and imagined what it will be like when success is the only option. You've made a commitment, the thing that will motivate you to stay on course. In **Clarity of Self**, you pay attention to what you're saying to yourself about yourself and make sure your inner dialogue affirms the unique you who is valued and worthy.

The **AAA**s of Mastering Resilience tie these concepts together, equipping you with a strategy to thrive in the face of any situation. When you're committed to your dreams and know your value, you're less likely to be swayed by others' inaccurate perceptions of you.

Resilience Reflection:

Think about an instance when you were thrown off by another person's assessment or judgment of you. Imagine that situation. What did you tell yourself at the time? Did you stand firm in your confidence, like Michelle? How did you talk to yourself? Did you beat yourself up? Ruminate or replay the conversation? How long did it distract you? How did you eventually move on—if you have—and what actions did you take?

Now imagine that you'd used the **AAA**s after that same scenario. Apply the **AAA**s right now to this situation.

What are you aware of? What plays out differently? How do you preserve your value and self-worth? How do you stay undiminished by the interaction? How do you effectively move on—because now you *definitely* do—and what actions do you take?

The **AAA**s can be used as often as you like. Since writing *Mastering Resilience: Transforming Into Your Purpose*, when the **AAA**s were first introduced, I've had many opportunities to use this strategy. It's quick and simple. The more it's used, the easier it becomes, the less you will find yourself in cognitively dissonant circumstances, and the more confident you will be.

SIX

Expect Bumps and Move Forward

*Sheri Chaney Jones, Founder of SureImpact
and Measurement Resources Company*

When Sheri Chaney Jones launched her software company, SureImpact, she faced the hardest time of her life. As she sourced funding for her latest entrepreneurial endeavor, she heard a question she never anticipated: "How can you have a family and be expected to grow this software company?"

Revolted by the inequality, Sheri grew depressed. In 2022, only 2 percent of US venture capital funding went to women founders (an even more staggering 0.9 percent of European venture capital funding went to women). But the explicit discrimination stirred up something even deeper—and more personal.

"Up until that point in my life," she says, "everything I'd ever done was about my own resilience. I'd grown up in a world where I knew I wasn't going to get the help or attention that I needed, so I developed this sense of self-reliance. When I launched the software company, I needed to find partners, whether financial or technology partners. I couldn't do it alone."

The company launched; there were customers. Yet, Sheri's depression worsened. Things got so bad that, one day, she found herself in the garage, putting her daughter's bike seat on her bike—and contemplating getting in her car and turning it on.

She sought counseling, and soon, she had a new clarity. "If I wanted to accomplish the goals that I wanted to accomplish in life, there were things about me I had to work on. And a lot of it had to do with the feelings of unworthiness and being unlovable, because I needed to change those feelings if I were going to be able to get people to help me."

Sheri Chaney Jones is the author of *Impact & Excellence: Data-Driven Strategies for Aligning Mission, Culture and Performance in Nonprofit and Government Organizations*. A self-described "serial social entrepreneur," she's an in-demand speaker on how mission-driven organizations can use data to solve complex social problems. She's the cofounder and CEO of SureImpact, a B2B SaaS platform that helps governments and nonprofits track, measure, and communicate their unique social impact, as well as the founder and chairperson of Measurement Resources Company, an organizational development and research firm that also serves government and nonprofits. Before founding SureImpact and Measurement Resources Company, Sheri had a ten-year career in government working for the Franklin County Juvenile Court and then the Ohio Department of Aging.

"Yes, I'm a business owner. Yes, I love to start things," says Sheri. "But what I'm starting always has an angle for moving social change forward."

Sheri's passion for solving large-scale societal problems started at a young age. She grew up in Ohio, the oldest daughter of an industrial designer father and a mother who struggled to demonstrate affection. "It was a very confusing childhood," she reflects, "but I didn't know it was confusing. It was normal. I think a lot of my drive to succeed was always to try to earn her love."

Sheri was a curious kid. "It makes complete sense that I grew up being a researcher," she laughs. When she was young, she wanted to create a lake in the backyard. She put potting soil in the backyard kiddie pool and added water. Disastrous? Yes. But her mother's reaction was disproportionate. As Sheri puts it: "There was a lot of shame around things that were part of my curiosity."

As a child, she was diagnosed with dyslexia. She endured a battery of psychological tests and received labels she didn't identify with. "I didn't understand these labels that people were putting on me. I felt very intuitive in terms of understanding the subject matter at school and understanding the world."

Then, at ten, she won an essay contest about what she wanted to be when she grew up. Her answer: an AIDS-curing pathologist.

However, the prize was tarnished. "I got to visit a pathologist and he told me you had to be really good at spelling to be a doctor," she recalls. "And so, he crushed my dreams—he didn't know this winning writer couldn't spell." Sheri sensed a purpose emerging in herself. Passionate about using data to predict things, she went into industrial and organization psychology. Her first job out of graduate school was helping people with severe and persistent mental illness find work—and "That changed my life forever," Sheri reflects. "I was using my love for data and prediction, and everything I knew about people and organizations, and I realized I could use what I was gifted at to make a difference in the social sector."

The more she worked in research and data, the more she discovered how her own positionality informs her passion. "I grew up a product of the seventies, where I was raised to believe that girls could do anything, and my gender didn't matter. Once I got into the work world and saw the real sex discrimination that exists, even today for women and girls, I think that's where my passion personally has come from."

> **Compassion for Self and Others:**
>
> Practicing compassion toward ourselves, as well as loving-kindness toward others, builds resilience in tangible ways. Responding with compassion—whether to our own stories or other peoples'—drives us to make the world a better place. Pg. 100.

Sheri is guided by that compassion in her work, in her volunteering, and, powerfully, in her personal life.

"Even though I grieve the nurturing I saw friends have with their moms, that wasn't my reality. Seeking her love developed in me a discipline to be high achieving. Maybe the motivation was wrong for the first twenty-five years of my life, but it did serve me very well. I'm a huge Tony Robbins fan. As he says: 'Thank you for giving me the act of forgiveness.'"

And that compassion belies an act of immense **cognitive reframing**, an element of Mastering Resilience that resonates with Sheri. "I had to do the **cognitive reframing** to bring myself out of a dark place and recognize that the adversity that I went through made me who I am today—and made me be successful. It's actually a gift, and that's a value of our company's."

Being super resilient, to Sheri, means not letting her adversities define her. "If you're super resilient," she says, "you keep going. When people ask that question—'Tell me your greatest failure,'—I don't know how to answer that. I haven't yet quit. I just keep taking the next right faithful step. You don't have to have it all figured out."

For someone hoping to master resilience and become super resilient, Sheri cites a recent aha moment. She was on vacation, hiking through the mountains in West Virginia. It was hot—really hot—and the trails were root-gnarled and rock-strewn, busy with insects and decked in spider webs. "I expected all those things," says Sheri. "They weren't annoyances to me. I wasn't like, how dare there be rocks in this path? That's a good analogy for life. If you just expect things will be bumpy and there will be challenges, you just keep moving forward."

> **The only way to fail is to quit.**
> —Sheri Chaney Jones

Connect with Sheri: https://measurementresourcesco.com/

Author's Note:

Early in her life, Sheri's drive for high achievement was fueled by her search for love. She knew she wanted to use her aptitude for research and data in the social sector, where her work could make a difference in people's lives. As her career developed, she recognized the gender-based discrimination she faced in the workplace, and began feeling compassion toward other women in her field. This, in turn, helped her experience compassion—and ultimately, forgiveness—toward her own mother. Sheri realized the value of adversity in her young life, and how it made her the unique and highly successful person she is today.

Compassion for Self and Others is a key element in Sheri's journey. It drives her personal life, work, and volunteering to this day. Her vision is to make the world a better place.

Compassion can be described as empathy in action, and the benefits of **Compassion for Self and Others** are overwhelming. Research suggests that feeling compassion for others deepens relationships, reduces stress, and improves physical and mental well-being. It increases resilience. Likewise, being on the receiving end of compassion boosts the immune system. The ripple effect of having compassion for yourself and others is endless.

What happens to our physical health and well-being when we lack compassion for ourselves and others, and carry feelings of bitterness, resentment, and anger, all while focusing on the negative? These feelings take a toll on the body and brain. The tie between emotions and the immune system is well established. Negative emotions weaken the immune system, which can lead to inflammation and physical health conditions such as high blood pressure, heart disease, and cancer.

This is the double-bind of negativity bias: If your perspective in life is full of bitterness, anger, and resentment, you'll find opportunities to be bitter, angry, and resentful time and time again.

Holding bitterness, anger, and resentment can become a habit that seems hard to break. After all, all of us are imperfect; all of us make mistakes. And negative self-talk is especially prevalent when we err. According to the Merriam-Webster dictionary, the word *mistake* means: 1) a wrong judgment, a misunderstanding, and 2) a wrong action proceeding from faulty judgment, inadequate knowledge, or inattention.

And yet, frequently, what we call mistakes can be opportunities for growth and deeper understanding. It's much easier to feel compassion when we realize the choice we made was due to incomplete information or attention. A coach once told me, "If you always do what you always did, you'll always get what you always got. If you don't like what you got, don't do it again." Though it may seem easier said than done, it's true.

As soon as you catch yourself focusing on the negative, you get the opportunity to change your inner dialogue to one of compassion for yourself and others. You can ask yourself: What good comes out of thinking about this situation from a negative perspective? How could it be different if I showed myself compassion? What would I do differently with this new perspective?

Having a daily compassion and gratitude practice will make compassion and gratitude a way of life. You will inherently treat yourself and others with understanding, patience, and loving kindness. According to Dr. Amit Sood from the Mayo Clinic, the pursuit of compassion will make you happier than the pursuit of happiness.

Resilience Reflection:

Think of a time when you believe you made a mistake. When I'm interviewing candidates for a job, my favorite question to ask is, "Tell me about the last time you made a serious mistake—and how you reconciled it." I've heard stories of coffeemaker mishaps, preschool drop-off snafus, disagreements that have ended friendships—you name it. (Of course, some people didn't admit they'd made a mistake at all!)

Now imagine that what you identified as a mistake was instead an opportunity to grow, to gather more information, to pay more attention, and to take a different action based on new knowledge. Imagine having compassion for yourself in that circumstance, showing loving kindness, patience, and grace to yourself. Do that right now. Take a deep breath and exhale a sigh of relief. What new insights do you have about your actions going forward? Write them down.

SEVEN
Recreating Health
Amanda Hinman, Founder
and CEO of Hinman Holistic Health

When Amanda Hinman was diagnosed with Hashimoto's thyroiditis during her fourth pregnancy, she was blindsided. Amanda had long made health and fitness her life's work. She taught cardio kickboxing classes two hours a day and had 13 percent body fat; salads and smoothies were constants in her diet.

"I remember feeling shocked," she says, "because this disease was described to me as something I'd manage for the rest of my life. I'd have to take medication. And once you have one autoimmune disease, you're more susceptible to others."

Amanda was rattled by the idea that her health could be declining. Then, eighteen months later, in the throes of taking care of a new baby, her eight-year-old daughter began having seizures—ten to fifteen a day.

"Anxiety was massively overwhelming her nervous system," Amanda says. "It was completely terrifying. There were many situations where I feared for her life."

Pediatric neurologists at Chicago's Lurie Children's Hospital told her the condition was genetic. Her daughter would likely be on medication for the rest of her life—twelve pills a day—just to manage seizure activity. She'd never be able to drive a car.

"Every single fiber in my heart and my being knew that could not be her future," Amanda says. "There's got to be something we're missing here."

Amanda Hinman is the founder of and lead practitioner at Hinman Holistic Health. For the past eight years, she and her team have been supporting women in their forties through sixties as they increase their energy, optimize their weight, and experience hormone and gut balance. What does that look like? Helping women feel more confident and understand the root cause of unwanted symptoms like weight gain, bloating, hypertension, anxiety, and more, so they have clarity on how to optimize their health.

"I do feel this pathway was kind of a divine redirection, if you will," she says. "It chose me as opposed to the other way around."

Her daughter's prognosis inspired Amanda to go back to school and become a certified functional medicine health consultant. "Functional medicine," she explains, "is understanding the root cause and upstream interconnected factors in our body systems where we have blockage, impairment, or depletion, that is creating a disease dynamic that's manifesting with symptoms." She discovered an autoimmune dynamic had created her Hashimoto's thyroiditis; a nervous system imbalance was creating her daughter's seizure activities.

Uncovering these dynamics was Amanda's first step. The next? A total transformation of her family's idea of health.

"It was a really beautiful chance to recalibrate," she says. "We were moving along at a pace in our lives that was just so busy, there was zero time to reflect. We never paused to think, 'How are we nourishing ourselves? What kind of meals are we eating?' I thought they were healthy because they were salads and mostly vegetarian, but they weren't holistic in nature—we weren't sitting down at the table being present together, connecting."

Changing their lifestyle and how they handled stressors, reducing environmental toxic exposures, sitting down to have conversations, and reprogramming their nervous systems with behavior change technologies—the transformation was enormous, and effective. In nine months, Amanda's daughter had weaned off all her medications and has been seizure-free ever since. Her own symptoms—exhaustion, acne, hair loss—vanished. It was miraculous, and for Amanda, not entirely unexpected.

"My faith has always led me to think that there is a silver lining, even in the most devastating circumstances. It's not easy," Amanda admits. "Trust me, when I was in the middle of it and shaking at night, I couldn't sleep because I knew within fifteen minutes of waking up, my daughter would start having seizures when her cortisol levels spiked. There were moments where it was terrifying. But I've always just had this knowing that this is happening for a reason."

Amanda understood her **BIG Why**.

Your BIG Why:

the future you create when success is the only option. Pg. 18.

Your BIG Why is living on purpose, for a purpose. Your calling, your *raison d'être*, your **BIG Why** is the impact you want to have on the world. It's nothing short of the legacy you hope to leave behind. In the Mastering Resilience formula, articulating Your **BIG Why** is the inspiration for moving forward, for letting the past be the past—and not pain affecting you today.

In her practice, Amanda guides clients on their own analogous journeys. After all, she has personal experience with the incredible resiliency of the human body. Her work with clients is physiological, psychological, and often spiritual.

"People come to me to look deeper," she says, "to explore the cause of a collection of symptoms." But tests and bloodwork are just the tip of the iceberg. "We get to look at what is happening physically in your body and see where there is a blockage, impairment, or depletion, and then look deeper to identify what causes the blockage, impairment, or depletion. This is usually something emotional, environmental, or behavioral. We make choices day in and day out that are influenced by our beliefs and our emotions."

And understanding the motivations behind those choices is especially critical during times of stress. This is something Amanda emphasizes with her clients. "We cannot avoid adversity in our lives. Recognize how significant stressors—whether it be relationship stressors, whether it be physiological stressors, whether it be situational—influence and inform our nervous system. Your nervous system is that central guiding light that impacts all functioning in the body: our mental capacity, our creative ability to interpret differently, our digestion, our immune system, everything."

It's not a coincidence to Amanda that the stress of a family member's descent into alcoholism precipitated her Hashimoto diagnosis.

Today, she encourages clients who are enduring emotionally

strenuous periods to prioritize balanced nutrition and exercise, to limit environmental toxins, and to get good rest, with the goal of reducing burdens to the body's systems. When there's trauma or adversity, "Can we minimize the toxicity the body has to deal with in other areas?"

Amanda's goal for her clients is that they feel inspired and empowered by the possibility of transforming their health. "Sometimes in the arena of health, it feels almost like a lack of choice," she admits. "So much of the work we do with women is redefining what creates a 'healthy life.' Not only does it get to be enjoyable, and uplifting, and fun—it *has to be* for you to build health and improve symptoms. We get to find the pathway where it doesn't feel like constant deprivation. You get to have clarity and understanding about what's going on. You get to have empowered choice and decision. You get to have prioritization of adding in pleasure, delight, joy, and fun variety, because when you do, that's when the body thrives.

"There's no better vehicle to recreate than the physical body," Amanda says. "Every single cell is constantly turning over. According to a new calculation by Ron Sender and Ron Milo of the Weizmann Institute of Science in Israel, your body replaces around 330 billion cells per day. That means your body is making over 3.8 million cells *every second*! The average woman has an entirely new skeletal system every seven years, new intestinal lining in six months, and a new liver in six to eight weeks. Your organs, tissues, and muscles are constantly changing because new cells replace the old ones. It's literally recreating itself. We get to tie that all together."

For Amanda, being super resilient is about a state of mind. "It's recognizing that life will bring challenges and having a willingness—not saying it's enjoyable or pleasurable—to embrace the challenges rather than try and resist. Because through those challenges is the greatest opportunity for reinvention. Resiliency is when we can learn to come back from adversity. Being super resilient means I'm not shying away from the next challenge. I'm not trying to avoid it. I'm actually, in a weird way, like, 'Okay, yep, let's go. Time to expand further.'"

Finding powerful meaning in adversity makes you super resilient, Amanda believes. For people who want to become super resilient, she encourages **cognitive reframing—seeing the good that comes out of adversity** and remembering **Your BIG Why.**

"What in your life are you struggling with?" she asks. "Is it inspiring purpose yet? Could it have an added benefit for others? That's the juice of life, when you see your adversity translating into helping and impacting others. That's what it's all about."

> **If you allow** your body to live with **different ch**oices in an environment **under a differe**nt set of circumstances, **it re-creates** itself differently too.
>
> —Amanda Hinman

Connect with Amanda https://www.hinmanholistic.com/

Author's Note:

Amanda's eight-year-old daughter was having seizures all day long. The seizures were so relentless that at night, Amanda would fall asleep—if she could fall asleep—knowing that it was just a matter of time before her daughter woke up in physical peril.

Inspired by her daughter, Amanda returned to school to study functional medicine and began overhauling her family's lifestyle. From the foods they ate, to how they ate them, to the toxins lurking in their home, Amanda changed how her family lived. When her daughter's seizures resolved themselves in a matter of months, Amanda knew it was time to share her knowledge with other women. That's when she founded Hinman Holistic Health.

Amanda was inspired by a **BIG Why**: the future you create when success is the only option. Having a **BIG Why** in life is crucial because it provides direction, inspiration, and meaning. It helps you set and pursue goals, makes challenges more manageable, and enhances your overall sense of fulfillment. Having a **BIG Why** guides your decisions, fosters resilience, and improves your well-being by aligning your actions with your core values and passions.

Your BIG Why is what's behind creating the ideal future you want for yourself. When you imagine this future, your **BIG Why** is the fire in your belly to make it happen. For Amanda, that fire was ensuring good health for her and her family.

Ask yourself: In the future, what difference do you want to make in this world? Who are you being? Who are you with? What are you doing?

The first step in the journey toward **Your BIG Why** is being honest about where you are now and all the things that got you here. This includes the experiences you've had, good and not-so good, which shaped who you are today.

I know I wasn't resilient, at least not at first, but I was able to cultivate resilience when I began my journey toward my **BIG Why**, acknowledging how far I'd come. When I reflected on how much I'd already been through and how much I'd already accomplished, I could see just how capable I truly was. Understanding my own capabilities motivated me and helped me define the future I wanted to create, one where I'd break the cycle of trauma to create a world where children, youth, and the adults that guide them thrive and are fulfilled in life.

Resilience Reflection:

Amanda's daughter's health condition lit a fire in Amanda's belly, transforming the trajectory of her life and the lives of countless others. Think about something you're passionate about, something deeply connected to your values. What lights the fire in your belly? Is it justice for children? The well-being of animals? Preserving and protecting our environment?

Now imagine that you take action inspired by that passion. What would you do? Take a moment to consider the unique impact that only you can make in the world—and take the next best step!

EIGHT
Breaking the Golden Handcuffs
Marietta Snetsinger, Founder of Ascend Franchise Solutions

Marietta Snetsinger grew up in Nova Scotia. As a child, she participated in 4H; riding horses was her escape from the turmoil at home. "I was always waiting for the other shoe to drop," she says.

Her parents' relationship was perpetually building toward divorce, creating an atmosphere of foreboding and impending doom. There were other burdens, too. Marietta's parents had adopted a boy with fetal alcohol syndrome, and he required an immense amount of their time and energy. The boy struggled, exhibiting dangerous, frightening behavior.

"I've kind of disassociated at this point," Marietta says. "I had to. He tried to burn our house down multiple times, and at one point, did so much damage that we had to move out for six months. Several times, he set our barn on fire. My horses, of course, were in the barn. I had a dog. He let the dog out. The dog got hit by a car and was killed. As a kid, I felt a lot of shame and bitterness."

As an adult reflecting on this early trauma, Marietta notes the hypervigilance—and fortitude—it bred. "I felt I needed to take care of my parents and manage all of that," she says. "I think about some of the things that I had to endure as a child, and I can see how they have shaped my strength now. If I could get through that, anything else I've faced is probably a lot easier."

She witnessed the true power of that strength when she graduated from university in the middle of a recession and started applying for jobs. "I knew what I wanted," Marietta says. "This was one of the first things I manifested, though I didn't know it at the time. I was future-pacing, fully embodying myself in that role. I wrote an acceptance letter that I was accepting the job—I don't even know how I knew to do that, but I did. And I ended up in the role."

That role connected her with someone in the franchise space in Ontario. Marietta spent the first part of her career as a field consultant. Field consultants work in franchise organizations, helping franchisees implement and embody the franchisor's business plan.

Marietta's gift was her ability to take complex situations and add a system and process to them. "I made sure [franchisees] were on board," she says, "and understood their role in the franchisor-franchisee relationship."

Yet, despite her aptitude for the work, Marietta found herself growing unhappy. She dreamt of starting her own business. "I wanted to be an entrepreneur probably my entire life, but I got stuck in the corporate, golden handcuffs."

When her position got eliminated, she received the most unexpected gift: a generous package. This was the impetus for her to start her own business.

"I thought, 'You're going to pay me that much money to go away? Great, I'll take it,'" Marietta says. "There's a really high failure rate of startup franchisors. Many of them really never get off the ground, and sixty-seven percent of them don't ever see a hundred units. That incubator time is so critical. I knew the knowledge I had of the business model and of the level of support required to set them up for success would be incredibly valuable."

Marietta Snetsinger has more than thirty years of experience in the franchise sector. For the past twelve years, she's run the consulting firm Ascend Franchise, where she specializes in teaching entrepreneurs how to convert their successful businesses to successful franchises. Based in Ontario, Canada, Marietta helps other people see their future potential and what's possible for them.

Throughout her life, Marietta has kept in mind her **BIG Why**, the guiding force behind her work. She wants to equip people converting their businesses to franchises to succeed—and help their future franchises succeed. After all, Marietta has decades of experience watching the franchise model "help people create incredible personal wealth. Someone who's working in a corporate role, maybe making $100,000, can step into a business opportunity where the sky's the limit. It's not just about money. It's about personal growth and opportunities available to people working within the organizations or their family members."

As a business coach, Marietta draws on her resiliency every day. After all, she describes being an entrepreneur as "not for the faint of heart—it's often either feast or famine." A few years ago, in one of the famine phases, she began leaning into other opportunities—including one with Thought Leader Academy. "I realized that part of what I do gets to be multiple revenue streams. I've been making peace with that and not feeling shame. We worry so much about what other people will think, when it's none of their business."

Marietta takes comfort in knowing her overall mission: "To help entrepreneurs. That might evolve and develop in different ways."

In her role as chief strategist at Thought Leader Academy, Marietta helps entrepreneurs—often coaches or consultants—to grow and scale their business. "Typically," she shares, "that starts with a book that lets them step into their own thought leadership. In many cases, that leads to a methodology or a process. They speak about it, which leads to engaging and building an audience that resonates with their messaging, which leads to monetizing and creating a program or a service to further support those people drawn to your brand, and how you can help them in their business or life."

Today, Marietta seeks community. What is a franchise organization if not a business community? She knows firsthand the impact of collaborating, cultivating **Connections and Close Relationships**. "As an entrepreneur," she says, "being in community can be the difference between thriving, growing, and scaling your business, or struggling in self-doubt. worry, and loneliness. And I can tell you, for the first five years of my business, I was not in those types of communities. When I began to embrace those worlds and those communities, and I found the right community for me, that changed everything."

> **Connections and Close Relationships:**
>
> encourage us to live meaningful lives, pursue our dreams, be ourselves, and keep going even when we want to quit. Pg. 158.

Marietta has seen how being in community can accelerate the process of implementation and action. With an accountability buddy, she's been hitting the keyboard every day for a morning writing session, working on her first book, *Ready Set Franchise*. "We do the thing that scares the bejesus out of us—that's where we get the transformation in our business, in our lives, and the confidence to kind of keep moving forward. You take the action, and the confidence comes after."

For Marietta, being super resilient involves insight, action, and acknowledgment. "You know what you need to do, and you find a way to make it happen—and it's not always easy."

Recognizing that the journey isn't always easy—that there might be house fires and layoffs—is key to Mastering Resilience. Marietta advises people to recognize the unpredictability of life and meet it with a degree of detachment.

"It's good to detach from what you think you know because it's not going to unfold the way you think. Be open to opportunities that present themselves, and don't be afraid. Sometimes it's worth taking that risk and doing it anyway."

> **Take the action.**
> **The confidence comes after.**
> **—Marietta Snetsinger**

Connect with Marietta: https://www.ascendfranchise.com/

Author's Note:

Marietta grew up with her share of fractured relationships. Yet, despite the turmoil of those early years, she has made a career out of cultivating and nurturing strong connections, growing a fulfilling professional network. She's always on the lookout for a potential collaborator or thought partner. As a business consultant and coach, she's committed to investing time and energy in teaching others to do the same. She knows the value of community; she knows the power of strong, mutually fulfilling relationships.

Positive, trusting relationships are essential to our well-being. When we surround ourselves with people who get us, who accept us warts and all, who celebrate us *and* our wins, who see the best in us when we might not see it ourselves, we feel seen, heard, and understood. It creates an atmosphere of trust, safety, and belonging.

And while it's comfortable to have superficial conversations about sports or the weather, having purposeful conversations with shared vulnerability has the potential to truly deepen relationships. When we foster strong **Connections and Close Relationships**, it also influences our long-term physical and mental well-being.

People who have close relationships have a more positive self-image, stronger immune systems, better cardiovascular health, and less depression and anxiety. Close relationships help us recognize, build, and strengthen our desire and ability to live resiliently.

On the other hand, social isolation, loneliness, and unhealthy relationships have a detrimental effect on our physical and mental well-being. According to the current US Surgeon General, Dr. Vivek H. Murphy's *2023 Advisory on the Healing Effects of Social Connection and Community*, "Poor or insufficient social connection is associated with increased risk of disease, including a twenty-nine percent increased risk of heart disease and a thirty-two percent increased risk of stroke. Furthermore, it is associated with increased risk for anxiety, depression, and dementia. Additionally, the lack of social connection may increase susceptibility to viruses and respiratory illness."

What kind of relationships do you want? You get to choose.

Furthermore, when we become super resilient, when we pay it forward, when we are the caring, dependable, loving, accepting person who believes in others, it makes all the difference in the world. High-quality **Connections and Close Relationships** lay the foundation for feeling valued. Life is more meaningful when we have them.

In my case, I had a high school Spanish teacher, Mrs. Camp, with whom I was very close. When I got in trouble for sassing the other Spanish teacher, Mrs. Camp welcomed me into her class. I used to stay after school and chat with her. She believed in me, encouraged me to go to college, and held space for my big emotions. To this day, I remember how she made me feel: wanted, worthy, and loved.

Resilience Reflection:

Take a moment to think about your own Mrs. Camp. Who believed in you and held space for your feelings? Who supported you no matter what? Was it a parent, a teacher, a coach? Likely, you remember the connection to this day.

How did you feel having a person who believed in you, cheered you on, saw your strengths, and put them to good use? How did you feel at the time? How do you feel as you think about that relationship now? Jot down an idea about how you can pay it forward.

NINE
The Laws of Water
Megha Bhouraskar, Founder of the
Law Offices of Megha D. Bhouraskar, PC

It was April 2001, and attorney Megha Bhouraskar was in her Empire State Building office, when she was interrupted during a deposition and told by her colleagues that she had to rush home. On her way to her building, the firefighters let her through the blockade because her colleague in the taxi told them that it was her apartment on fire. She lived with her son and her husband on the twenty-fifth floor of a building overlooking the East River. Beneath their unit, she learned, a man was growing marijuana with a shoddy grow-light setup: hot lamps and cheap wooden boards.

"When they started to ignite, the building superintendent didn't call 9-1-1," Megha says. "They tried to have the maintenance workers put out the fire. They left the windows open, and our window above was ajar. The fire experts later told us our apartment was so filled with carbon monoxide that one flame made our entire apartment explode. My computer flew out the window, twenty-five flights down. The apartment was unrecognizable. It was one black hole. Nothing survived."

At the time, Megha's son was in school; her husband had been working at home but fled the apartment just in time. "Overnight, we had nothing other than what we were wearing that day," she says. "We didn't have a home."

Devastating as the fire was, it was, in a sense, a stroke of luck.

Megha's marriage had been deteriorating for years—perhaps it had even been over before vows were exchanged—but her husband refused to separate. "I'd been going around praying to God," she says, "that some major interference would make the difference so that I wouldn't have to initiate the divorce. And then lo and behold . . ."

With their home razed and their possessions destroyed, Megha and her son went to live with her parents; her husband refused to join them. Within a few years, the couple was divorced, and Megha was rebuilding her life.

Megha Bhouraskar is an attorney and consultant. Since 2012, she has overseen and operated her own law firm, the Law Offices of Megha

D. Bhouraskar, PC, which draws clients from the global Indian diaspora. Prior to founding her firm, Megha was a partner at a large law firm, where she established the Bollywood industry in America and represented top Indian media companies, including RPG, Tips, and Eros, while also working on copyrights and trademarks, real estate, and litigation.

In her consulting, Megha mentors individuals and businesses—from established companies to startups—assisting with strategizing, negotiating, and transformation. She's the author of *How to Have a Business Presence in the U.S.A.* and the creator-host of the podcast *She Warriors — New York.*

Though she describes herself as having "one foot in New York and one foot in India," Megha is hesitant to attach much significance to fixed identities, such as wife or daughter. "In an Indian cultural con-text," Megha says, "not being married, not having lived a very sort of traditional lifestyle, that identity I've had to rework years ago. Some-times I think we get trapped in identities that are created for us."

Megha's parents were from India; they'd come to the United States when Megha's father received a postdoctoral fellowship in economics at Princeton and subsequently joined the United Nations. Working at the United Nations afforded the family a good life, rich in travel. Megha herself was born in Ethiopia when her father was stationed there for several years. They returned to New York City and fell into a rhythm—spending the school year in the States, summers in India.

"I became very comfortable with being in India," says Megha, "and also very comfortable in New York." She also became comfortable with her parents' expectations about what career she'd have and who she'd marry: "Somebody Indian, somebody who they could relate to."

While she was at Barnard College, Megha became friends with a journalism Ph.D. student at Columbia University, who'd grown up in New Delhi. "A circle of us were good friends," says Megha. "And eventually all our friends started marrying off or getting jobs, and there was more talk in my home about me getting married or what I was going to do next. And my dad was very clear, in my fourth year of college, he said to me, 'A man can leave you. Somebody can take your money, but nobody can take your education and what you are capable of doing. Is it going to be lawyer, doctor, or engineer?'"

Megha was flummoxed—she'd been studying fashion management on the sly in her last year of college, to the detriment of her grades. She went from being on the Dean's List the first three years to a sudden drop in her fourth year. She quickly ruled out the math and science required for med school and engineering and chose law.

Soon, her father was asking about the LSAT, pushing her to apply for law school.

Amidst the confusion and upheaval, Megha sought stability. She'd learned her journalist friend was talking to common friends about marrying her. "I don't think we were very romantic with each other," she says, "nor were we in love. But we did share a friendship and common interests like film, music, and literature. He was very progressive—I knew there'd be no issues with me working or doing any of the things I liked to do."

As the two spent more time together, Megha's parents pointed to an upcoming trip to India, suggesting the couple get married.

"I remember calling him," says Megha, "he was working in LA. I called him up and said, 'Mom and Dad say we should get married if we're hanging out together so much. What do you think?' And he said, 'That sounds great.'"

The wedding was in Delhi in December. Megha's mother traveled ahead of Megha to make preparations because Megha was in her second year of law school at the time. "It was a big fat Indian wedding," says Megha. "I didn't participate in terms of choosing anything I was wearing—I showed up like a doll." Eight days of events, parties, and dancing. The wedding brought Megha and her husband's friends from all over the world.

The night the festivities were over, Megha and her new husband sat in a café in the hotel where they had a suite, eating "bullseyes," vanilla ice cream enrobed in dark chocolate. In the middle of a bite, her husband paused.

"Do you think we rushed this?" he asked. "Was this a mistake?"

The emptiness had been echoing within her since the hoopla ended. Still in her red sari, Megha jumped up and left the café. "I ran across the hallway to the elevators," she says. "It's a very fancy hotel—marble staircases and marble floors—and I'm in all my gold and finery, my husband comes running after me, but he's a journalist and sees one of the most famous actors walk into the lobby. So, he got detoured and started talking to him—I went upstairs. It was not a romantic night at all."

Though they both knew the marriage was a mistake, they never spoke about it.

"He went back to LA. I came to New York," Megha says. "My being married gave me a license in the Indian context to just be myself." The two lived their separate, amicable existence, ensconced by their community of Columbia-Barnard friends, until the question of children arose.

"He wasn't ready for that," Megha says. "I insisted. Then I had some trouble getting pregnant or sustaining the pregnancy, but eventually had my son. That's when things really started to break apart. Now I was expecting my husband to be home at a certain time and help out."

By the time her son was six, Megha was pushing for a separation. She wanted another child; her husband didn't. "He was really not present as a father," she says. "I didn't want my son perpetuating that, thinking that was acceptable. I figured it was better for him not to have to see that and feel it. So, I started to suggest to my husband that we separate, but he refused."

After the apartment fire, Megha told her parents she couldn't endure the "farce of reestablishing a home with the wrong man." She watched her son become happier without the marital tension. But even after the divorce was finalized, there were challenges.

"The most disturbing piece was the financial piece," Megha shares. "I was raised very traditionally, and my mother never earned, and my dad took care of everything. So, as much as I earned and as much as I did, I always gave my money to my husband, and I assumed he was managing it properly. Instead, it turned out he'd created all this debt I wasn't aware of. All the money I got from the insurance company after two years of litigation had to go toward paying the debt. So, I was totally broke. It was starting from scratch."

Sometimes the very things that have hurt us, the adversity we've faced, and our journey are the very things that will give people hope and a purpose. Pg. 18

And yet, Megha believes in everyone and everything having a purpose, or a **BIG Why**. Even the most challenging circumstances offer important insights.

For too long, she realizes, she had disassociated herself from the money she was earning. "There's something to be said for being pro-active instead of just waiting for some major incident to happen," says Megha. "Not that I could have anticipated the fire, but I wasn't doing anything about a bad marriage or getting out of it because of the social pressure—the huge Indian taboo around divorce."

Megha compares being super resilient to a flowing stream. "I see resilience as water," she says. "You flow, you keep your inherent consistency, which is water, but you understand the paths that are open to you, and you go down those paths trusting that those are meant to be. And when there are rocks or a mountain or something, you understand whether you're meant to flow around it or over it or under it."

She encourages people who are cultivating resilience in their own lives to trust. "Trust in the universe," says Megha. "To trust in the universe, you have to trust in yourself. Trust in the fact that you are special, that you're here for a special purpose or many purposes. And know that even if you're in a bad state, if you trust that it's meant to be better, it will be better. The universe has your back. The universe doesn't punish. The universe will show you ways."

> **To trust in the universe, you have to trust in yourself.**
> —Megha Bhouraskar

Connect with Megha: https://www.mdblawoffices.com/

Author's Note:

Megha was stuck in a languishing marriage when her New York home exploded. Literally. Being forced to leave her apartment also forced Megha to leave a marriage tacitly governed by Indian cultural norms. Indeed, she would come to view the fire as a message from the universe, spurring her to take an action—getting divorced—that she, otherwise, might not have been ready to take.

The right path isn't always a smooth path. After Megha's divorce, she found herself in litigation and dealing with unforeseen debt. And yet, she continually trusted in herself and the universe. The adversities she'd overcome in the past created her future. After all, that fire destroyed more than just her apartment. It gave her hope. Purpose. A **BIG Why**. The journey led her to center her work as an attorney on championing women, and to set up and build successful businesses.

Megha believes in *everyone and everything* having a purpose.

Many of us already have a vision for our future. We're inspired to make a tangible impact. But when we get caught up in the busyness of life, it's easy to lose sight of our **BIG Why**. Sometimes it takes a metaphor from the universe to open our eyes.

In one season of my life, I was so consumed with work that I was clocking sixty-hour weeks, including the weekends. This went on for months. Powering through project after project, I was the living embodiment of workaholism.

One weekend, I was able to steal away on a family trip to the mountains. While sledding with my youngest child, I broke my leg, and not just your run-of-the-mill break—a trimalleolar fracture. When I was rolled into the ER, the nurse announced, "We got a deformity!"

After surgery and the weeks of recovery that followed, I came to a realization: I needed to slow down. I was so focused on the day-to-day that I'd lost sight of my purpose. I'd lost sight of the important things in life. Having the downtime let me reflect and make a course correction. Now I could refocus on the things that were most meaningful in my life.

Resilience Reflection:

As Steve Jobs said in his 2005 Commencement Address at Stanford, "You can't connect the dots looking forward . . . you can only connect them looking backward. So, you have to trust that the dots will somehow connect in your future. You have to trust in something—your gut, destiny, life, karma, whatever. This approach has never let me down, and it has made all the difference in my life."

I didn't connect the dots until I *had* to, until the universe stopped me in my workaholic tracks.

Think of a time when the universe offered you an opportunity to "connect the dots," to look backwards and recalibrate moving forward. It may've been an illness or injury; it may've been a relationship change, a job loss, or a rejection. (I like to think of rejection as redirection.)

Consider: Did you use this opportunity to "connect the dots?" To reflect on what you trust in or value, what you want to shape your future? Or did you write it off as an inconvenience or worse?

Now imagine you get to create a story that ascribes positive meaning to the challenging experience. Imagine that telling this story—and believing in it—will make all the difference in your life. Write that story. Do you feel more empowered? Does connecting the dots show you a deeper message? Experience a sigh of realization in your body.

TEN
I Wanted to Know
What Happiness Was
McKenzie Buzard, Founder of McKenzie Hypnosis

From the outside, McKenzie Buzard's middle-class childhood looked normal enough . . . certainly not traumatic or emotionally abusive. Yes, she came from a blended family: Her mother had been divorced twice before marrying McKenzie's father. And, yes, there were four half-siblings dealing with addiction or early pregnancy, though they were older, out of the house, and living with their own fathers.

McKenzie was born in Portales, New Mexico, and raised as an only child by a mother who, she says, had "a very restless spirit." They moved around at her mother's whims twelve times before McKenzie left for college. "My mother had depression, possibly bipolar, and narcissism. She was always searching for happiness. But she was searching for it in different places, thinking that changing the location would make things better."

McKenzie's domineering mother clung to her youngest daughter. She homeschooled her, preventing her from forming close relationships with her peers. "She wanted to keep me close," McKenzie admits. "I didn't have much say over who I was being formed to be. The emotionally abusive piece was, because she was depressive, I was wrapped up in her emotions. From an early age, I was the one trying to fix that. So, I became an overachiever, I became a perfectionist, all those things that stem from trying to be the one who keeps everyone happy."

McKenzie Buzard is a certified hypnotherapist who helps people transform their past trauma and limiting beliefs into new, more empowering beliefs. While her practice is based in Castle Rock, Colorado, she conducts virtual hypnotherapy sessions for clients around the world. A rapid transformational therapy (RTT) practitioner, McKenzie specializes in a modality of hypnotherapy that combines neural linguistic programming and psychotherapy. Trained at the Hypnosis Motivation Institute, she works with people dealing with depression, anxiety, addictions, and phobias, as well as with people who want to increase their confidence, understand themselves better, love themselves more, and, ultimately, move toward more happiness and fulfillment.

McKenzie's interest in self-improvement is deeply personal. Growing up, she witnessed the effects of her mother's moods. She recalls walking on eggshells around her mother, something she saw in her father's behavior, as well. "My father was very much a shy, kind of quiet person," she says, "and my mother ran the whole dynamic. It was an uncomfortable environment to live in, volatile all the time. Then you bring in my siblings, their addictions, their depression, their children. At points, we had to take in their kids and help raise them."

McKenzie knew there was another way to live. "Very early on," she says, "I knew that I needed to get out, to make this change, to be different. It was a lot of unhappiness, and I wanted to know what happiness was."

Clarity of Self:

being sure about what you like, what you don't like, your values, your talents and abilities, your character, etc.—all designed to identify who you get to be to make your impact in the world.

Pg. 66.

When McKenzie left for college, she embarked on a journey of self-development. From traditional talk therapy to tapping, psychedelic experience, and faith-based work, she sought experiences that would help her understand human emotions and what drives them, as well as how she could better herself and transform.

Having experienced profound transformation herself, McKenzie is passionate about helping others achieve the same. One of the ways she does this, as an RTT practitioner, is by working with clients to change limiting belief systems and scripts.

"We first look for root cause," McKenzie explains. "Say someone comes to me with anxiety. At the beginning of the session, after taking them into a hypnotic state, I regress them back to where that anxiety started and why. The mind is so intelligent. It can take you back to those memories. What we're looking for is the belief system that was placed in that moment. Often, anxiety goes back to a childhood experience where you were embarrassed, or something happened that made you feel bad about yourself, and made you think, 'I need to do things differently. I'm not good enough as I am.'"

After determining their limiting beliefs, McKenzie facilitates a re-programming to change the subconscious script running in the client's mind. "If we find that you have a belief that you're inherently different and you don't deserve good things in life, we reprogram that to say, 'I do deserve good things in life. I can connect with people around me.'"

The initial reprogramming takes place during one hypnotherapy session. Afterward, McKenzie gives clients a hypnotic recording to further ingrain those new beliefs and habits. "It takes twenty-one days for you to create new neural pathways in your mind," McKenzie shares. "On a very scientific, physical level, when we're changing belief systems, we're creating new neural pathways in the brain. Whether it's tied to anxiety or negative spirals or a sugar craving, a neural pathway is just a route your mind has always taken. With the recording, we're training it to think—and behave—differently. As you listen in a hypnotic state, you're very suggestible. In that state, your subconscious takes positive affirmation statements as fact. It helps you circumvent the part of your brain that says, 'Oh, that's not true,' and starts to integrate those concepts a lot faster."

In her own transformation, McKenzie has combatted her own damaging scripts. "'I'm different. I'm not enough. Who am I? I am in this alone. Who am I to go and make these connections? Why would people ever want to acknowledge me?' A lot of disempowering stuff."

Even though she's worked through those limiting beliefs, McKenzie still faces challenges. She counts running a business as a major personal development tool for anyone.

"I build relationships with clients through one-on-one referrals, so there are times when it ebbs and flows. I see all my fears coming up, even the ones that I usually have under control." In those circumstances, she revisits the principles of Mastering Resilience.

"I've also become a pro at **cognitive reframing**," McKenzie says. "I ask myself, 'Why is this showing up, and what is this here to teach me? Where do I need to pivot, and how can I use this to propel me forward?' You have to do this in business a lot. I look at every obstacle as something that's here to teach me something, to help me grow."

And growth is what being super resilient is all about, in McKenzie's experience. "It's taking whatever has happened to you—whether that's trauma, adverse experiences, heartbreak, setbacks, letdowns—and using that to grow, to learn, and to become a stronger, better person."

She ties this back to cognitive reframing. "Saying, 'Yes, this happened, but what did I make it mean? Can I make it mean something different? Can I use it to empower me instead of using it to knock me down even further?' You always have that choice. Where you find resilience is in making a different choice about what it means about you, what it means for your life, and what it makes you believe."

For people who are on their own journey to combating old scripts or damaging beliefs, for people who are on the road to becoming super resilient, McKenzie encourages people to be open-minded and inquisitive, especially about themselves. "Get curious—without judgment—about everything about yourself. As you continue to understand yourself, make that conscious choice to choose something different. I think that's where resiliency starts—having the courage to do that."

> **Why is this showing up and what is it here to teach you? Look at every obstacle as something that's here to help you grow.**
> **—McKenzie Buzard**

Connect with McKenzie: https://www.align-and-thrive.com/

Author's Note:

As the youngest in a blended family, McKenzie lived a tumultuous childhood. Her mother's mental illness manifested in a stifling codependence with her young daughter, as well as an unceasing restlessness—the family moved twelve times before McKenzie began college. She grew up walking on eggshells around her mother. Meanwhile, her older siblings struggled with addiction and early pregnancy. Often, they'd come to live with her and her parents. There wasn't much happiness.

But McKenzie took initiative. The challenges she experienced compelled her to go on a journey of self-discovery—to seek happiness. This journey proved transformational. She got to know herself better and, in turn, discovered her calling to help others do the same.

Despite growing up as a people pleaser and a perfectionist, McKenzie arrived at **Clarity of Self**. She knows herself, her strengths, her beliefs, and with that awareness, she holds herself in high regard. **Clarity of Self** cultivates self-esteem, and that's part of why it's so important for becoming super resilient—knowing and understanding what makes you uniquely you, serves as a catalyst for creating your ideal future state (**Your BIG Why**).

When you know your values and behave in line with those values, you're more likely to keep commitments to yourself (**Your Why NOW**). Being rooted in your authentic self allows you to make choices that move you forward toward your dreams and goals. It becomes easier to set boundaries because you can trust yourself to make decisions that are in your best interest.

When you're not clear about who you are, it's easy to morph into an identity based on what other people think of you. Many people do this, especially those who have been deeply criticized or cut down. Having clarity of self allows you to gauge whether those around you also have your best interest in mind.

Resilience Reflection:

Most of us have behaved against our better judgment to please another person. Think of a time when you acted in a way that didn't align with your values to appease someone else—a time when, afterward, you thought, *That's not like me.*

How did you feel? What caused you to act out of character? Were you aware of people pleasing in the moment, or did it occur to you after the fact? What were you experiencing at the moment?

Now imagine yourself making a different choice, one where your actions are in keeping with your values. How would you feel in the moment, speaking up for yourself? Would there be any discomfort? Would it pass? How would taking a stand benefit you in the long run? Write it down, and identify your next best step.

If you know that you have a people-pleasing tendency, make time every day to examine whether you've fallen into the trap. Identify steps you can take to set better boundaries for yourself."

ELEVEN
Mental Toughness for Life
Sheryl Kline, Founder of The Zone Lab, LLC

In 2015, Sheryl Kline landed her first public-speaking event. "A C-suite staff friend of mine asked if I would sit on a panel," she says. At the time, Sheryl was a mental-toughness coach, known for her work with young athletes, kids, teenagers, Olympians, and professionals. So, when her friend asked her to be on the panel '50 of the Most Promising Women in Technology,' Sheryl balked.

"I was a little bit terrified, to be honest, but I did it. I had to prepare and get over my fear."

The event went so well, Sheryl wound up with a new client base. "I started helping women be highly influential under pressure and receive funding for their companies," she says. "Before, they'd crack under pressure during high-pressure conversations with (Venture Capitalistists) VCs."

Working with female leaders and executives, Sheryl realized her coaching—around clarifying vision, building confidence, cultivating tools to influence leadership and increase impact—could benefit other women, too. She decided to focus her entire coaching practice and speaking career on mental toughness and high performance for women in the workplace.

For two years, Sheryl studied with an NFL player turned playwright and expert storyteller, who teaches stage presence and speaking. Under Bo's tutelage, Sheryl created a declaration of ambition: "I am going to speak at the United Nations someday," she says. "Pretty crazy, considering I was not an experienced speaker yet."

But Sheryl was laser-focused. At first, she spoke anywhere that would have her (for free and for modest fees)—at her kids' tennis team, Corporations' lunch-and-learns. As she established herself, she soon received (paid) invitations to speak at Fortune 500 companies on topics such as "How to Defuse Emotionally Charged Conversations and Remain Highly Influential." Finally, in August 2023, she was invited to speak at the United Nations' leadership summit.

Sheryl Kline is a mental toughness and certified high-performance coach. For more than twenty-five years, she's worked with Olympians and world-class athletes, female leaders and their teams in San Francisco, Silicon Valley, and across the United States. In addition to now being a sought-after speaker, she's conducted workshops and training for enterprise clients. She's the bestselling author of *Zoned In: The Mental Toughness Required for a World-Class You*, and the founder and CEO of The Zone Lab, a leadership training course for female leaders and male allies featuring her signature Limitless Leader Roadmap curriculum. Sheryl is a mother of three, as she puts it, "amazing adulting kids."

"Many times I share similar wisdom with my kids and my clients about the same things," she says. "Operate as if success is inevitable, and then work backward from there."

Consider the Possibilities:

Setting goals and visualizing them hugely impacts your likelihood of achieving them.

Pg. 142.

What led Sheryl to her fascination with mental toughness and high performances? A formative childhood experience. When she was ten, Sheryl was called into the principal's office at the small private school she was attending. She walked in and found her parents. Despite her hard work and "What I thought were good grades," Sheryl says, the principal warned her that she wasn't meeting expectations. She was put on an academic probation.

This was frightening. Sheryl began working harder than ever. She viewed the school as a refuge from the chaos she called home.

Raised in an upper-middle-class family in the San Francisco Bay Area, her mother suffered with bipolar disorder and her brother—ten years Sheryl's senior—struggled with addiction. This particular school, says Sheryl, "In my ten-year-old mind was my ticket to being happier than my mother and not struggling like my brother."

Despite her hard work that year, come June, Sheryl's dad called her into the kitchen while he was making breakfast and broke the news—She wouldn't be returning to the school in the fall.

"That was really devastating for me," says Sheryl. "It imprinted in my mind that I wasn't good enough, because I did everything I could to work longer and harder, to be in that school. After I transferred, I started wondering, 'Who gets to decide who's good enough?' I was working hard, and I was getting good grades. Why was it up to my principal? So, I became interested in world-class athletes and Olympians because they chose themselves to be the best."

Sheryl's focus remained on high-performance athletes until that first speaking invitation. As her clientele shifted, she discovered something about female leaders that resonated with her own story. "What I was finding is that the voices of female leaders are not being heard, valued, or respected enough with their leadership," she says.

That reminded Sheryl of her own mother not being heard in her home.

"Growing up," Sheryl says, "my mom was very passionate about owls. She loved owls, one species in particular. But whenever she'd talk about these owls at home—why they're important, why she wanted to save them—my dad would say, 'Who are you to save a species?'"

Sheryl's mother passed away at the age of sixty-nine. Three months later, the species of owl went extinct.

"That really solidified in my mind that women have a different level of intuitiveness, compassion, and ability to lead with love. There's a special spark placed within all women and men, but women are more likely to be voiceless, because of cultural reasons, social indoctrination. My story is really about my mom. Her voice was extinguished way too early, and so was her passion."

As Sheryl's business continues to grow, her goals are no less lofty than leveling the patriarchy. She launched the enterprise version of her curriculum, The Fearless Female Leadership, aiming to reach ten thousand new clients in 2024, and she's motivated by the idea of giving back. "I have a motto and an affirmation I speak to myself every morning," says Sheryl, "that I'm shooting for this revenue goal because the more I earn, the more I can live and the more I can give.

I have clear giving goals. And so, my revenue goals are really tied to impact."

Sheryl's impact—on her clients and the people she's touched through her talks and her books—is immeasurable. What makes her super resilient today, she says, is being "finally able to practice what I preach, taking a dream and turning it into reality, helping others take negative emotions and turn them into fuel."

And becoming super resilient often involves shifting the perspective wherein fear or failure *does* become fuel. Being super resilient means having "the ability to make peace with failure and the emotions that come along with it," Sheryl says. "Honor the emotions and decide to move forward. Without honoring them, looking them in the eye, and making peace with them, it's difficult at best. Emotions are powerful— they're like a bully ten times your size. You can't push them out of the way, so you might as well make peace with them."

To make peace with emotions and build resilience, Sheryl offers a concept from her curriculum: the ECO Mindset. ECO stands for empathy, curiosity, and optimism.

"You need to have strategic empathy for yourself," says Sheryl. "If you fail or have a negative emotion, rather than say, 'I am so frustrated with myself,' say, 'I notice.' When you say, 'I notice,' it creates some space, it creates distance. When you say, 'I am,' you're creating a label and accepting it as truth, and you'll keep doing the things you don't want to do because you've accepted that you *are* that negative emotion. If you can go from 'I am' to 'I notice,' then you can observe it, take a breath, and say, 'What's my next best step?'"

> **If you can go from 'I *am*' to '*I notice*,' then you can observe it, take a breath and say, '*What's my next best step?*'**
> **—Sheryl Kline**

Connect with Sheryl: https://www.sherylkline.com/

Author's Note:

It's not every kid who gets kicked out of elementary school who becomes fascinated with Olympians. But being put on academic probation ignited Sheryl's obsession with high performance. While she first focused on athletes, she grew more and more interested in executives, especially women, whose goal-setting know-how positioned them for success.

Sheryl practiced what she preached on her own path to becoming a public speaker. Setting a "declaration of ambition," she operated like success was inevitable—and acted accordingly. It's no surprise that she was booked to speak at the United Nations.

Goals are at the core of **Consider the Possibilities**, and as a mental toughness and certified high-performance coach, Sheryl is a verified expert at not only setting goals, but also achieving them. She's helped everyone from pro athletes to Silicon Valley founders to do the same. And Sheryl knows that visualizing goals—making them tangible, specific, and clear—is essential to achieving them.

Over the years, I've made several vision boards. One of them had a few images and lots of words:

"What's your story?"

"Write a book."

"The book is written."

"One door."

"Mission complete."

I took a photo of the board, printed it out, and taped it inside a cabinet. I opened and shut the door of the cabinet easily five hundred times over the next several years, but along the way, I stopped noticing it; the vision board became part of my scenery.

One day, I opened up the cabinet door and took a look at the photo for the first time in months. I paused, focusing on the words.

Hey, I wrote that book!

That program I'd envisioned was created and exists to this day—One Door Any Door™ is a program that facilitates easy access to mental-health resources where access coordinators help clients navigate complex systems to get the care they need. Back when I'd made the vision board, did I have a clue about publishing a book or implementing a program that was a glimmer in my imagination? No. But gradually, the vision became clear and the path appeared one step at a time.

Resilience Reflection:

Sheryl warns against using "I am" statements to affirm a negative identity. Here, I want you to reclaim "I am" and use its powers toward envisioning your goal.

Think of a goal that you would *love* to achieve. Maybe you want to be a seven-figure CEO. Maybe you want to found a camp for underprivileged children. Maybe you want to run a marathon. Maybe you want to earn a college degree. Whatever your goal is, write it down.

Now create an "I am" statement of yourself as the person who achieves this goal.

I am a seven-figure CEO.

I am a founder.

I am a marathoner.

I am a college graduate.

But it's not enough to just say "I am." Now you get to imagine what it looks like to *be* this person. Allow yourself to feel the emotion attached to the goal as if you already achieved it. Imagine the sense of accomplishment, the feeling of excitement, and the thrill of celebration.

In that frame of mind, create a representation of you achieving that goal. This could be a screensaver or a picture. For the next thirty days, close your eyes for sixty seconds per day and visualize yourself achieving your goal—accomplishment, excitement, celebration, and all!

TWELVE
I Deserve to Be Happy
Juliana Garcia Halloran, Nutritionist BSc

Juliana Garcia Halloran grew up competitive and athletic in Houston. From an early age, her father cultivated her fierce spirit. "He would put me up against my cousins a lot," Juliana recalls. "He'd say, 'My daughter can outrun your son.' I didn't mind because I would beat out the boys sometimes, and it fed my ego. I was very athletic at a very young age."

At the same time, her father was verbally and physically abusive to Juliana, her siblings, and her mother. Home did not always feel safe. "I was in a very toxic environment," Juliana says.

Sports provided an outlet, and Juliana began competing when she was seven. By the time she graduated high school, she was weighing athletic scholarships that she ultimately turned down. Juliana became pregnant at nineteen, and she knew she would raise her son as a single mom. Her resilience kept her strong and provided support. For a time, she moved in with her own mother, who'd by then divorced Juliana's father.

All the while, Juliana was conscious of breaking the cycle.

"I wanted to make sure my son wasn't in the same kind of environment," Juliana says. "I spoke to him differently than I'd been spoken to, treated him with loving kindness and positivity. I worked multiple jobs so we could move into a nicer neighborhood with a better school district." Not only did she work multiple jobs—Juliana completed her BA in psychology by the time her son was five; she even competed as a semi-pro basketball player.

Her athleticism and competitiveness brought Juliana to personal training, which she began when her son was ten. A few years later, she discovered the world of competitive bodybuilding. Her love for the sport was near instantaneous. "I'm very competitive with myself," Juliana says. "What I loved about bodybuilding was that it was a competition between me and the person in the mirror."

And there were endless hours in the mirror, with Juliana spending days in the gym either training her clients or working toward her pro card. Bodybuilding enhanced her personal training—it taught her about physiology and the fundamental importance of nutrition.

Eager to learn more, she went back to school to earn a degree in nutrition science. "I didn't realize how important nutrition was, that what you put in your body to create that physique is really what mattered." Bodybuilding and studying nutrition, Juliana says, "has made me better equipped to help my clients."

A couple years after Juliana began professional bodybuilding, she got married. By this time, her son was sixteen. The family lived in Texas, but the relationship was fraught. Issues plagued the couple, and within seven years, they divorced. Juliana's husband moved to Chicago, and soon Juliana realized they were revisiting their relationship. As messy and complicated as that was, she was open to this. After all, despite everything, she still saw her ex-husband as her soulmate.

When she left Texas to live in Chicago with her now-ex, she still thought there was a chance. Juliana tried to go on with life as usual. Training kept her grounded, and she was training for one of the biggest events of her bodybuilding career, a pro bikini bodybuilding show with the International Federation of Bodybuilding.

IFBB competitions are what bodybuilders like Juliana call "our Olympics." After training for nearly a decade, earning her pro card and beating out other women in her class at qualifying shows across the country, Juliana felt good about her prospects at the IFBB show. But in the midst of training, she faced a serious problem. Her husband asked her to leave the house.

Clearly, things between the couple had gone afoul in the past—but asking her to leave the house was a new low: "The most heated time of our marriage," Juliana says.

She considered skipping her competition, staying, and fighting for the relationship. But something within her couldn't abandon that person in the mirror. Plus, her son was rooting for her; he encouraged her to stay in the competition.

"I decided to stick with it and not give up," she says. "I'd made an agreement with myself. It took a lot for me to make that decision, and it was scary. It almost paralyzed me."

> **Commitment:**
>
> The definition of commitment is an agreement or pledge to do something in the future. Pg. 58.

Juliana Garcia Halloran is a professional bodybuilder in the International Federation of Bodybuilding. A former semi-pro basketball player, she's worked as a personal trainer since 2004. In addition to training individuals and coaching amateur bodybuilders, Juliana is a nutrition coach—teaching clients to make behavioral changes to their lifestyle by implementing mindset shifts.

After he asked her to leave the house, Juliana knew she had to break ties with her ex. "I made an agreement with myself that I deserve to be happy, and if this person doesn't want to be with me, I can't force that. I needed to be brave enough to make that exit."

It wasn't easy. Juliana filed for bankruptcy—she was in debt, she'd been living paycheck to paycheck—and in 2019, she moved to San Clemente, California, to start over near her son.

Her commitment to living her best life motivated her.

Today, after four years of rebuilding, she's back to training for her next competition. She's personal training and nutrition coaching, too, helping clients with weekly calls and frequent messaging on an app. "We set goals, talk about what their meal plan looks like, and create a shopping list. It's an integrative plan where you're just changing these behaviors and creating a new lifestyle." And undergirding this plan are critical mindset shifts.

"It's hard for people to understand that they have total control," Juliana shares. "A lot of times they say, 'I've tried everything. Nothing works.' I help them switch their story, to see that the things they do will lead to something healthier. Then I find out what their barriers are. We look at those and figure out how we can overcome them."

Between childhood abuse, divorce, bankruptcy, and moves across the country, Juliana has experienced her share of barriers and demonstrated boundless strength in what she's overcome. After she left her ex and moved to California, Juliana secured a job at an elite fitness club as a head trainer, only to be let go when the COVID pandemic hit several months later.

"That's when I transitioned to my virtual coaching," she says. "That year, I decided to just take care of myself and not worry about anybody else, and it really made me stronger. I was on antidepressants. I was on Lithium. I decided I needed to get off of them [under the care of a physician] and try to rebalance myself, which I did. I started to feel like myself and better, and I did a lot of healing that year. I was at home by myself in an apartment with my dog and trying to establish myself in my business, as well."

Today, Juliana's business is thriving. "Starting over almost four years ago," she reflects, "and knowing what I know now, I would do it a hundred times over. I'm in a beautiful relationship with a man who has an amazing daughter, and I'm thriving now."

Between bodybuilding, coaching, personal training, and nutrition coaching, plus the marketing and branding work that goes along with it, there's constant activity. "I've established relationships," Juliana says. "What I'm doing is coaching them on how to live a healthier lifestyle that's sustainable."

What makes a person super resilient? According to Juliana, it's about having the ability "to overcome things—regardless of what's going on in your life—in a safe way, understanding that this is temporary and that if you just keep putting one foot in front of the other, that some good can come out of it." But being super resilient also means "acknowledging the help you might need—and not being afraid to reach out for support."

In her work supporting individuals working toward their health and fitness goals, Juliana knows the power of being present and committed when someone feels stuck. And that's her biggest piece of advice (beyond moving every day, at least ten minutes after each meal)—It's okay to feel stuck.

"Remember, it's temporary," she says. "Make a plan and find support. Do what you need to do to get your freedom and your happiness back."

> **Do what you need to get your freedom and your happiness.**
> **—Juliana Halloran**

Connect with Juliana: https://julianahalloran.com/

Author's Note:

For Juliana, bodybuilding is a personal challenge—she calls it a competition between herself and the person in the mirror. And competition has long been about more than winning races or collecting trophies for her. As a child, channeling that competitive drive into sports allowed her to overcome the difficulties she faced at home, building her resilience muscles in the process.

When Juliana found herself in a dissolving marriage, on the eve of the IFBB competition, she faced a tough choice. Leaving her house could mean losing her marriage. And yet, her resolve was firm—She'd made a commitment to that strong woman in the mirror.

While this path took her through bankruptcy and other major challenges, knowing that she'd bet on herself kept Juliana going. Indeed, the fact that she respected her commitment to herself allowed her to persevere and create a new life of authenticity, alignment, and joy.

What empowered Juliana to take that big leap and head to the IFBB competition? Her **Why NOW** motivated her to keep going and stay on track, heading toward her dreams.

It's easier to say, "I'm committed," than to *be committed*. **Your Why NOW** puts the action in the present moment, where your commitment is no longer an idea or a daydream. And your commitment paves the way for an action plan. Whether or not you're committed is evidenced by the steps you're taking toward realizing your goal. **Your Why NOW** gets you moving. That's the only way your vision can be achieved.

Resilience Reflection:

I've long wanted to run a marathon. It's no secret—I've told people that I'm going to do it, I've imagined myself crossing the finish line, and I've even researched training schedules. I like to run! And yet, I've never truly made the commitment. I may have *felt* the sense of commitment, but I didn't implement a plan of action to make those 26.2 miles happen.

If I'm serious about committing, it's time to do something.

What have you thought about doing that you haven't acted on? What commitments have you expressed and not followed through on? Without judgment, make a list of these ambitions, goals, or even far-fetched ideas. Take a few moments to reflect. Are these aims still aligned with your values or your sense of self? If not, can you let anything go? If these aims do still correspond to the person you are, now is the time to explore what's preventing you from taking action.

What is it costing you *not* to take action? Consider what's possible if you act on one of these goals today. What will be better or different when you take action? How will your commitment change your life today, tomorrow, this year, next year, and five years in the future? If you're serious about committing, it's time to do something!

THIRTEEN
Lessons in Growth from
'The Most Organized Man in America'
Andrew Mellen, Wall Street Journal-Bestselling Author and Founder of Andrew Mellen, Professional Organizing

In 1996, Andrew Mellen was laid off from a theater he'd been running in Seattle. For years, his life had been devoted to theater, and on the day he found out, he felt his world upended. Fortunately, he soon got a gig co-producing an awards ceremony at the Kennedy Center.

One of the awardees was a Nobel Peace Prize winner, and Andrew went to his office to collect photographs to create a slideshow to be displayed during the ceremony. The photography files were a mess. Things were misfiled, mislabeled, and several key images had been lent out and never returned. After several hours rooting around in the file cabinet, Andrew pulled together a collection of images. He was ready to leave when the awardee's wife invited him to stay for a soda and a conversation.

She asked who he was. He told her his story: He was in his late twenties, and he'd been working in theater since college. He told her about the layoff, the Kennedy Center gig, and the slim plan—to move back to New York after the awards ceremony was over and see what came next.

The awardee's wife listened. Then she asked Andrew if he'd like to organize their photographs.

Andrew was honored and thrilled at the chance to spend time in the Nobel Peace Prize winner's orbit. He eagerly agreed. They arranged a date for him to begin in December.

He moved to New York only to have the couple postpone the date until January, then February, and then March. In the meantime, he found pick-up work copyediting for large and small publishers, all while continuing his search for another administrative position with a theater—either as a director or in another creative role.

When March rolled around, the assignment was postponed again, this time indefinitely. So, while in fact, he never ended up organizing their photographs, in the interim, something else happened.

"In those four months, I told every person I met, 'I've got this great gig. I'm going to create a comprehensive photographic archive for a Nobel Peace Prize winner.' That led a friend of mine to refer me to her accountant, who needed a filing system built. So, I built that filing system for the accountant, and then the accountant started referring her clients to me."

Looking back, this was a time of big transitions. He was starting a new solo practice as a professional organizer while also producing and directing a play off-Broadway. But he discovered that he was no longer satisfied with his theater work.

"That last play was a miserable experience for me for several reasons," he admits. He remembers, "Standing on my stoop, talking to a friend about how not satisfying that production was for me, and saying, 'I'm going to put the theater work on a shelf for now and see how far I can take this organizing thing because I'm making money. I'm solving problems. My clients are very happy. And I don't have any of the struggles in this work that I had hustling for gigs, auditioning—all of the things that come with show business that have nothing to do with making art. I don't have any of those hassles to navigate. It's just me and the client.' That was the pivotal moment for me."

Today, Andrew Mellen is an established professional organizer—the media has dubbed him "The Most Organized Man in America." He's the author of the *Wall Street Journal–* and *Audible*-bestselling *Unstuff Your Life!*, as well as the Amazon number-one bestselling *Calling Bullsh*t on Busy* and *The Most Organized Man in America's Guide to Moving*.

For more than twenty-six years, he's been a sought-after coach with highly recognizable clients and a speaker on stages from SXSW to TEDx. As founder and CEO of Andrew Mellen, Inc., he designs seminars, programs, and virtual courses that combine mindfulness practice, neuroscience, and a bit of common sense to help people transform their mindsets and simplify their lives.

Perhaps the role that chance has played in his own life has given Andrew a flexible perspective on personal narratives. After all, though he grew up enjoying the game Concentration and, later, as a director and producer, excelled at taking disparate elements—actors, designers, scripts—and "[turning] them into a cohesive whole"—though he brought the principles of "like with like" and "one home for everything" into his organizing work—he never set out to mastermind a career in organization. That work was simply the next puzzle to solve.

The first puzzle that challenged Andrew? "Interpersonal interaction," he says. "How do you connect with other people? How do you relate to other people? What does friendship mean? Who can be counted on? What do they expect of me?"

Those questions arose in his Detroit childhood, where he endured bullying by several girls cheered on by neighboring boys. Their harassment confounded him. "I allowed them to bully me because the alternative was to do something that I had been told was wrong [hitting girls]. I didn't know how to navigate a situation like this. Something's happening that is very wrong, but the only solution that I can think of is also not on the table."

Adding to that growing sense of confusion was his parents' fractious marriage. When he was twelve, they divorced. By fourteen, he was self-medicating with drugs and alcohol, he says, "To find my way through adolescence and navigate the disintegration of my family."

It took sixteen years for him to put the substances down and get sober. In that span of time, he had traveled the country, acting anywhere he could find work—from regional theaters to touring the country performing improvisational theater in prisons and living on a school bus. By his late twenties, theater was what he knew how to do well and his vocation, and his commitment to the art brought him to a critical decision.

He had just finished a long run of a very physical comedy in Cleveland, *Vampire Lesbians of Sodom*. "After the play closed, I was in a friend's studio, stretching out on the floor," Andrew says. "And I was having difficulty touching my toes. Remember, I had just finished a four-month run of pratfalls and tumbling in four-inch stiletto heels, and I got concerned that my drug and alcohol use was about to interfere with my ability to do my work as an actor. My physical flexibility was one of my assets as an actor, and I got very concerned that I was doing something that could compromise that. Because the only thing that really mattered to me at that time was my ability to support myself working in the theater."

That was the turning point for Andrew. He returned to New York and asked his then-boyfriend, who was active in a recovery program, for support. "'I want you to find me one of those meetings you go to.'"

Andrew sees a familiar link between the psychology behind recovery and decluttering. "If you think about it, it's not drugs and alcohol themselves that are the problem. They only become a problem when I ingest them," he says.

His clients face similar circumstances.

"Typically, people are stuck, immobile, and that's usually when they find me. They have the desire for change. And they've probably tried to get organized in the past," he says. "What they haven't tried is to change how they think about, feel about, and interact with stuff. That's what sets me apart from other organizers. I coach my students and clients to recognize that clutter is a symptom—even though it might present as the problem—and that until they shift themselves in relation to these physical items, no solution is going to be sustainable. The solution isn't focusing on the clutter—it's focusing on yourself and how you relate to stuff. Once you do that, you're on the path to setting yourself free."

Throughout the Mastering Resilience process, mindset shifts are critical to helping people move beyond adversity and trauma, and the stories they breed. And that sort of **cognitive reframing** is integral to Andrew's ethos. Across his work, whether in books, seminars, or individual coaching sessions with his clients—who range from overwhelmed stay-at-home parents to CEOs and ultra-high-net-worth individuals—he addresses "those limiting beliefs and that static mindset where possibility is not possible yet."

He continues to examine his limiting beliefs, as well. "I work pretty diligently to meet those stories and acknowledge them, then dismantle them, reject them, or set them aside. I've been lucky to have a few great mentors in my life who have encouraged me to do things that I didn't think possible, and then to leverage those experiences internally the next time I face a similar challenge."

Connections and Close Relationships:

Have a mentor or trusted coach or advisor . . . because they *are* or have *been* where you're going. Pg. 156.

Andrew has transformed the offer of an unexpected organizing gig into a full-scale virtual and in-person empire.

"The business these days is itself a puzzle I'm intrigued to solve," he says. "We are *growing* a business, present tense. I don't think you *grow* a business once, and then you get someplace. There isn't a single static outcome. So, I do what I can to gamify the experience for myself so that it never feels like a life-or-death proposition, as if my survival as a person is hanging on the business remaining successful and growing. That keeps it fun and keeps my work in perspective."

Growing, of course, is at the heart of becoming super resilient, as Andrew sees it.

"When I think about what it means to be super resilient, it's not taking things personally. It's having enough of a sense of self coupled with a strong survival instinct that says, 'This won't kill me. And if it won't kill me, what's the worst thing that could happen?' I might not enjoy how it feels in the moment, but the quickest way to not feel this way for long is to meet whatever is happening and address it in that moment. Walking away from it or denying that something is happening is only postponing any sort of sustainable solution and resolution."

For someone whose work is steeped in mindfulness, it's not surprising that Andrew invokes spiritual parables. Jesus in the desert, Buddha under the Bodhi tree—both realized eventually that, "Everything is perception and often a fiction borne of my imagination. Seeing it for what it really is means I can either give it credence or poke a hole in it on my journey toward enlightenment. What we think and feel are as real as we allow them to be. And just because I'm perceiving or experiencing something in this moment doesn't mean that it's true or that it will always be this way. If I don't like what's happening or how I'm experiencing it, I can always change it."

> **If I don't like what's happening or how I'm experiencing it, I can always change it.**
> **—Andrew Mellen**

Connect with Andrew: https://www.andrewmellen.com/

Author's Note:

As a child, Andrew struggled to trust people. He remembers how difficult it was to forge friendships and how painful it was to be bullied by his peers while his parents' marriage fell apart. By the time he was fourteen, he was using drugs and alcohol to cope. Eventually, as his substance abuse interfered with his work, he turned to his then-boyfriend, who helped him find a recovery community. Slowly, Andrew learned there were people he could count on.

As his connections with others grew, Andrew found himself able to navigate difficult career changes, seeing them for the opportunities they were. Developing dependable interpersonal relationships was no longer so challenging. Instead, Andrew gravitated toward people who inspired him to dismantle his limiting beliefs and take risks in his career.

Today, Andrew does the same for the hundreds of thousands of people he teaches and mentors through his speaking engagements, writing, and coaching.

We know that **Connections and Close Relationships** can have a tremendous impact on our physical and emotional well-being. Simply put, meaningful relationships can prolong our lives. And, as we see in Andrew's story, they can also help us tackle those limiting beliefs. In other words, they're beliefs that aren't useful.

It doesn't take a team of mentors to help. In fact, one good person can make all the difference. Maybe that person is a friend, a teacher, or a colleague; maybe it's a neighbor or a coach. So long as that relationship is one of compassion and understanding, free of judgment and overreaction, it can help you break through those limiting beliefs.

Resilience Reflection:

Identify a limiting belief, something you routinely tell yourself about yourself that isn't serving you and isn't true. Maybe you criticize yourself for not spending enough time with your partner; you might call yourself a bad spouse. Maybe you consider yourself a chronic procrastinator; you might call yourself a failure. How is this belief holding you back?

Now find one person who has achieved what you would be able to achieve if this belief weren't holding you back. Maybe this person is in a fulfilling marriage. Maybe this person is a go-getter, someone who accomplishes what they set out to do. Even if the person is a public figure, you can still learn from them—read about them, watch interviews, and note common denominators. If it's a friend or colleague, take them out for coffee and ask questions about how they did it (i.e., crushed their to-do list, celebrated twenty-five years of marital bliss).

Based on what you've learned, what does this person do differently from what you're doing?

Choose one of this person's actions or behaviors to incorporate into your own life. If it worked for someone else, it can work for you. Success leaves clues, and this reflection will allow you to receive mentorship even if you don't know the person.

Bonus: Go a step further. Make a "dream mentor list" and begin to cultivate a relationship with at least one person on that list. Start with generosity—buy their book, like their posts, subscribe to their podcast, and then, when you're ready, ask them to mentor you.

FOURTEEN
Clearing the Air
Molly Jones, President and CEO of Jones Design Studio

Twenty years ago, Molly Jones was in the midst of a professional existential crisis. She'd been an architect for her entire professional life, and, as she says, "I was no longer enjoying it." What she did enjoy was learning about sustainability (architecture that creates and sustains a healthy environment), but when her employer organized Leadership in Energy and Environmental Design (LEED) training for its employees, Molly was overlooked.

As her disillusionment with her profession grew, so, too, did her concern about the spaces people inhabit. And for Molly, that concern was deeply personal. Her parents' house had had a leak in the secondary bathroom. When it was repaired, they waited years to replace the water-damaged carpet in the adjacent hallway.

"I was starting to learn about sustainability in the work I was doing," Molly says, "and I told them, 'You really need to get a disaster restoration company to come in and help you mitigate this properly. Of course, they didn't listen—they just had the carpet people pull it up and put new carpet down.'"

When the old carpet was removed, Molly's mother, who suffers from chronic obstructive pulmonary disorder (COPD), went into an exacerbation so serious that she spent weeks in the ICU. Suddenly, she needed to be on oxygen.

"That was a turning point," Molly says. "Most people don't understand the importance of indoor air quality, especially people who have lung diseases and disorders like COPD or asthma. It's super important to understand the health impact of what you bring into your house—the finishes and paints you choose, how you filter your air, and what kind of flooring you use. And it really got my attention. I decided, 'This is what I want to do.'"

Being overlooked for that initial sustainability training was, as Molly puts it, "a speed bump along the way." Having determined her **BIG Why,** or the force inspiring her transformation, she educated herself, obtained certifications, and, within a few years, was the director of that firm's sustainable facility program. "That was really the beginning of where I'm at today," Molly says.

BIG Why:

You must know **Your BIG Why** to determine your target, your true North, before beginning any journey. Pg. 19.

Today, Molly Jones is the president and CEO of Jones Design Studio, PLLC, a women-led design firm based in Oklahoma and Arkansas. With a focus on environmental stewardship, Jones Design Studio draws on Molly's deep expertise in federal sustainability.

Beyond sustainability consulting, Jones Design Studio acts as an owner advisor in the design-build space. "The design-build project-delivery method allows project teams to really bring innovation to those projects and how they approach the problem the project is trying to solve," says Molly. "That's what we love to do. It allows us to bring our sustainability expertise into the development of project goals and requirements. We still do a lot of sustainability consulting, but we're really focused on building our owner-advisor services. We're considered a nontraditional architectural firm because we don't actually practice a lot of architecture."

A dog and cat mom, she's been married to her wife for twenty-eight years. She's also working on her first book about how the choices people make while building can potentially mitigate climate change.

Molly learned how to achieve practically anything she set her mind to early in life. She grew up in Ohio, the oldest of four girls in a middle-class family. Her father worked as an accountant; her mother also worked part-time while raising the children.

From a young age, Molly loved animals. "It was because I could connect with them better than people," she says, "because I was afraid. I was afraid of who I was. I was afraid of my sexuality. I was afraid I'd get caught or I'd be outed. Somebody would figure it out somehow. And so that put a shroud of fear over me growing up. As I got older, I realized I could be accepted if I excelled at everything I did, so I poured all my energy into being the best at whatever it was I was doing."

Winning state gymnastics competitions, running cross country, flourishing academically and artistically, Molly continued hiding her sexuality and racking up bona fides—as she puts it, "fear cloaked in achievement."

It was after Molly had finished college that her parents found out about their daughter's sexuality. "It was really difficult," she says, "because I was outed by a relative and then subsequently disowned by my father, so I basically didn't have much contact with my family for ten years. I didn't get to control when I came out or under what circumstances. I didn't get to own my story."

It's no wonder, then, that Molly is so committed to infusing her work with her values, to bringing herself to her work in intentional and public ways. This was a choice she made early on and consciously.

"I came to this realization reading *Zen and the Art of Making a Living* as I was beginning to really explore my profession and find a spiritual home within the Buddhist tradition," Molly says. "I studied Tibetan Buddhism for quite a number of years. It introduced me to the idea that I can have a flexible mind. Architects are problem solvers, so we can distill things down to their essence and provide elegant solutions. I became interested in how I can unleash my mind, especially the subconscious mind, and allow the core of who I am to permeate the work that I do."

While Molly's experiences—of first living closeted and then being outed—were difficult and, at times, painful, her **clarity of self** underscores what those years gave her: the opportunity to intentionally reveal herself in her work and the ability to achieve.

"Learning how to achieve was really, really helpful," Molly says. "That's a gift I don't know how I would've gotten otherwise, as early in life as I did. It doesn't help me as much today, but it helped me get to where I am. It helped me along the way. Even though it came out of a place of fear and not feeling safe at home, it helped me break through fear. I was driven to do and to achieve whatever I wanted. To this day, fear doesn't stop me. I feel the fear and move through it."

And that's what makes Molly super resilient: "Not letting the stuff that happens in my life—and that happens in everyone's life—stop me from doing whatever I want to do." That attitude is born, in part, of the "flexible mind" that Molly has cultivated through decades of studies in Tibetan Buddhism, meditation practice—at least an hour a day—and a tremendous amount of mindset work she continues to do daily.

Molly defines super resilience as "tenacity with contentment." And for people working to master resilience in their own lives, she offers advice that echoes the potency of that definition. "Your life is a reflection of what's going on inside of you," Molly says. "If you don't like what's going on in your life, look inward. If you change your mind, you change your life."

> **Be afraid and do it anyway; feel the fear and move through it.**
>
> **—Molly Jones**

Connect with Molly: https://www.jones-design-studio.com/

Author's Note:

Early in her life, Molly learned how to achieve. She excelled in academics, sports, and art. But even as a young person, she suspected she was using her drive and talents to garner the approval of her family. Perhaps it was a subconscious means of distracting them from her sexuality, which she feared they wouldn't accept.

As an adult, Molly continued to identify as a high achiever. So, when she was overlooked by her employer for the LEED training, it was a professional existential crisis. Today, she refers to this experience as a "speed bump" along the way to where she is now. Not only did she create the business she owns, she is an advisor in the design-build space, and an author.

Molly views her future from the perspective that success is the only option. Her passion for sustainability, for the health of a building's inhabitants, as well as its environment, inspires her stewardship. And the principles of Tibetan Buddhism that she studied for years underpin her firm's ethos.

Your BIG Why is your foundation for becoming super resilient in any area of your life—be it your profession or career, relationships, business, or leadership. Having clarity about your own vision guides you on your resilience journey and helps drive your commitments, decisions, and choices. In other words, **Your BIG Why** inspires the vision you have for your legacy.

Resilience Reflection:

By now, you've had the chance to think about the impact you want to have on the world. And you've probably started to realize how that impact begins with what's happening within you. As Molly says, "If you change your mind, you change your life."

While the elements of Mastering Resilience are all interconnected, I can't help returning one last time to the **BIG Why**. The **BIG Why**, after all, is your inspiration. It's what you want for your future self. It doesn't have to be a global cause or a massive commitment. It's what you focus on, what inspires you to take action toward your dreams and goals.

Take a few moments to reflect on your beliefs and values. What is the inspiration that keeps you moving onward and upward? What is your vision for your future self? If you know **Your BIG Why**, write it down.

You might recall my experience creating a vision board from my notes on Sheryl Kline's story. Now, it's your turn. Make a vision board or another visual that makes your aspirations tangible. Create the roadmap to your legacy.

CONCLUSION

The people profiled in this book are extraordinarily ordinary. I know that might sound paradoxical, but it's true. Every single individual I spoke to made extraordinary choices in the midst of adverse circumstances. The specifics may vary, but again and again, the people I talked to shared stories of tough childhoods, emotional hardship, professional struggles, heartache, and loss. These are the ordinary elements of a human life. In other words, these super-resilient people are people like you and me.

I hope these stories of becoming super resilient leave you astonished and inspired, and remind you that you don't have to be a celebrity, or an Olympian, or a Nobel Prize–winner to live an extraordinary life.

An extraordinary life is one that's future-focused, not stuck in the past. An extraordinary life is one of purpose and meaning. As renowned trauma therapist Judith Herman, M.D., writes, "The survivor who has accomplished [their] recovery faces life with few illusions but often with gratitude . . . [They] have a clear sense of what is important and what is not."

Everyone chronicled in these pages has overcome adversity and emerged with clarity and purpose. And while I consider them super resilient, I know all too well that there are many, many, many super-resilient people in this world.

The **Resilience Reflections** in this book are intended to move you along on your journey toward super resilience. Whether you're reflecting on what inspires you, devising mindset shifts, or identifying your commitments, these reflections will give you practical strategies for recognizing and honoring your extraordinary self.

I want you to know that you can do this. You can take what has happened to you and use it as motivation to achieve your dreams and goals. You can create the life you want to live. It's a day-by-day process, one I hope you always stay focused on. Return to these stories for a boost of inspiration. To reconnect with your values. When you're seeking a deeper understanding of how the elements of Mastering Resilience apply to YOU. Along the way, YOU get to remember your potential. YOU—yes, YOU—can become super resilient.

ACKNOWLEDGMENTS

First and foremost, my deepest gratitude goes to the fifteen extraordinary individuals who shared their stories in this book. Your willingness to revisit difficult moments from your past and reflect on the resilience, strength, and determination that shaped your success is an inspiration. Your journeys remind us that adversity does not define us—what we do with it does.

A heartfelt thank you to my developmental editor, JoAnna Novak. Your skillful and compassionate approach to these conversations made it possible for my colleagues to share their experiences with honesty and vulnerability. This book would not be what it is without your talent and dedication.

To my publisher, Patti Fors, and Muse Literary—your unwavering support, belief in my work, and steadfast friendship have been instrumental in bringing this book to life. Your commitment to this project has meant more than I can express.

To my immediate family—my husband, Gary, and my adult children, Tess and Rae—your relentless love fuels me to pursue my dreams and goals. Your support, encouragement, and belief in me are the foundation of everything I do. Thank you, and I love you. To my grandson, Kallen – your arrival clarified why resilience outlives the moment and becomes a legacy.

As Maya Angelou so powerfully said, *"I can be changed by what happens to me. But I refuse to be reduced by it."* This book is an expression of that truth.

Finally, to the readers—may these stories serve as a testament to what is possible, no matter where you begin.

ABOUT THE AUTHOR

Lorry Leigh Belhumeur, Ph.D., is a bestselling, award-winning author of *Mastering Resilience: Transforming into Your Purpose.* A renowned resilience expert and visionary in children's mental health and wellness, she is a fierce advocate for breaking multi-generational cycles of adverse childhood experiences (ACEs) while mitigating their negative impact and setting those who experienced ACEs and other adversities on a trajectory toward success.

Dr. Leigh Belhumeur's career began with teaching psychology full-time at Mount Saint Mary's University and advanced through roles in inpatient mental-health facilities, teaching college and graduate students, private practice, and ultimately to community mental health. Her personal challenges with ACEs fuel her passion for helping others, leading to initiatives like community training on ACEs and her team's development of the RESET (resilience-building) Toolbox during the global pandemic in partnership with local agencies.

A sought-after speaker and subject matter expert, Dr. Leigh Belhumeur delivers impactful training on resilience, toxic stress,

ACEs, and trauma-informed care. She is a TEDx speaker on ACEs and resilience, and her award-winning book *Mastering Resilience* informed the creation of the Super Resilient Youth curriculum. Her insights have shaped conversations at national and international levels, influencing policies and practices that support healing and empowerment.

As the CEO of a multi–eight-figure nonprofit, she has led the organization through more than a decade of exponential growth, proving that mission-driven leadership can create lasting systemic change. Her leadership extends beyond organizational growth: She is committed to systemic transformation, ensuring that resilience-building resources reach those who need them most.

Dr. Leigh Belhumeur also supports individuals and businesses on their own journey to *Becoming Super Resilient* through Super Resilient CPR and other resilience-building strategies and programs.

OTHER BOOKS BY
LORRY LEIGH BELHUMEUR, Ph.D.

MASTERING RESILIENCE
Transforming Into Your Purpose

MASTERING RESILIENCE
Transforming Into Your Purpose WORKBOOK